The Cold War:
Core Documents

The Cold War:
Core Documents

Selected and Introduced by

David Krugler

Ashbrook Press

Library of Congress Cataloging-in-Publication Data

The Cold War: Core Documents;
Selected and Introduced by David Krugler

p.   cm.
Includes Index
1. United States – Politics and government.

ISBN   978-1-878802-37-8

(pbk.)

Cover images, above the title, left to right:

Kennan, George F. Portrait, 1947. Harris and Ewing Collection, Library of Congress, LC-DIG-hec-12925.

Truman giving Truman Doctrine address, March 12, 1947. Courtesy Harry S. Truman Library & Museum. Accession number: 59-1252-3.

Margaret Chase Smith, 1943. Library of Congress, LC-USZ62-42661.

President John F. Kennedy Delivers Address on the Nuclear Test Ban Treaty, July 26, 1963. Abbie Rowe, White House Photographs. Courtesy John F. Kennedy Presidential Library and Museum, Boston. Accession Number: AR8046-C.

President Reagan addresses the Nation from the Oval Office on National Security (SDI Speech), March 23, 1983. Courtesy Ronald Reagan Library. Accession Number: C13574-22A.

Cover image, below the title:

Confrontation at the United Nations, October 25, 1962: Deputy National Photographic Intelligence Center Director David Parker points out the photographic evidence while US ambassador Adlai Stevenson (at right) describes the photos. USSR Ambassador Valerian Zorin is presiding at far left. The Dino A. Brugioni collection at the National Security Archive; reproduced from www.nsarchive.org with the permission of the National Security Archive.

Ashbrook Center at Ashland University
401 College Avenue
Ashland, Ohio 44805
www.ashbrook.org

About the Ashbrook Center

The Ashbrook Center restores and strengthens the capacities of the American people for constitutional self-government. Ashbrook teaches students and teachers across our country what America is and what she represents in the long history of the world. Offering a variety of resources and programs, Ashbrook is the largest university-based educator in the enduring principles and practice of free government. Dedicated in 1983 by President Ronald Reagan, the Ashbrook Center is governed by its own board and responsible for raising all of the funds necessary for its many programs.

Visit us online at Ashbrook.org, TeachingAmericanHistory.org, and 50coredocs.org.

Contents

General Editor's Introduction

This collection of documents on the Cold War continues the Ashbrook Center's extended series of document collections covering major periods, themes, and institutions in American history and government. The volume begins with George Kennan's "long telegram" from Moscow in 1946 that laid out the terms of the containment policy that the United States would follow in various forms throughout the struggle with the Soviet Union. It ends with the transcript of a phone call between President George H. W. Bush and German Chancellor Helmut Kohl in 1989 in which the two leaders discussed how to deal with the changes transforming Russia and bringing the Cold War to an end. It covers American aid to Europe in the early years of the Cold War and American intervention in subsequent years in conflicts around the world to contain the spread of Soviet power. Its documents also explore the domestic effects of the Cold War, chronicling how national security concerns affected relations between American citizens and between Americans and their government. This collection and its companion volumes – *World War I and the Twenties*, *The Depression and New Deal*, and *World War II* – comprise a detailed account of the major events of America's 20th century.

When the series of Ashbrook document collections is complete, it will be comprehensive, as well as authoritative, because it will present America's story in the words of those who wrote it – America's presidents, labor leaders, farmers, philosophers, industrialists, politicians, workers, explorers, religious leaders, judges, soldiers; its slaveholders and abolitionists; its expansionists and isolationists; its reformers and stand-patters; its strict and broad constructionists; its hard-eyed realists and visionary utopians – all united in their commitment to equality and liberty, yet all also divided often by their different understandings of these most fundamental American ideas. The documents are about all this – the still unfinished American experiment with self-government.

As this volume does, each of the volumes in the series will contain key documents on its period, theme, or institution, selected by an expert and reviewed by an editorial board. Each volume will have an introduction highlighting key documents and themes. In an appendix to each volume, there will also be a thematic table of contents, showing the connections between various documents. Another appendix will provide study questions for each document, as well questions that refer to other documents in the collection, tying them together as the thematic table of contents does. Each document will be checked against an authoritative original source and have an introduction outlining its significance. Notes to each document will identify people, events, movements, or ideas that may be unfamiliar to non-specialist readers and will improve understanding of the document's historical context.

In sum, our intent is that the documents and their supporting material provide reliable and unique access to the richness of the American story.

David Krugler, Professor of History, University of Wisconsin–Platteville, selected the documents and wrote the introductions, notes, and study questions. David Tucker edited the collection; it was copyedited by Joan Livingston. Ali Brosky, Sarah Morgan Smith, and Ellen Tucker provided editorial support. Lisa Ormiston oversaw production. This volume was made possible by the generous support of Dick Uihlein, Uline, and other Ashbrook donors.

David Tucker
Senior Fellow
Ashbrook Center

Introduction

The Cold War lasted for almost a half-century, from the mid-1940s through the early 1990s. The conflict's origins were deep and complex, but the root cause of this persistent hostility between the United States and the Soviet Union was ideology. The United States is a constitutional democracy. This form of government, along with capitalism, abundant resources, and advanced industries, made the nation an unmatched global power by the end of World War II. The Soviet Union (officially the Union of Soviet Socialist Republics or U.S.S.R.) was the world's greatest communist state. Arising amid the growing pains of industrialism in the West, communism is an ideology antithetical to democracy and capitalism. Communism seeks to erase the class lines inherent in capitalist societies. To accomplish this goal, the Soviet Union completely denied or severely restricted its citizens' basic rights: freedom of speech and press, property ownership, and the free practice of religion. American democracy was imperfect – at the start of the Cold War, racial segregation and prejudice denied millions of African Americans their rights – but the principles of individual freedom and equality made possible movements to dismantle state-sanctioned discrimination during the Cold War itself. In the Soviet Union, totalitarian rule in service to communism rarely wavered.

Yet these vastly different nations had joined together during World War II to fight a common foe, Nazi Germany. This fact alone reminds us of the complexity of the Cold War. The alliance did not abate the possibility of postwar conflict. It increased it. Distrust and suspicion based on each nation's respective actions pitted the two superpowers against one another. Both sought to spread their respective ideologies and forms of government. As they competed for allies, they pulled much of the world into the conflict. The label "Cold War" refers to the fact that the United States and the Soviet Union never directly went to war with one another, but proxy wars in Korea, Vietnam, and Afghanistan, among many places, demonstrate the long and devastating reach of the conflict.

The Cold War did more than determine international alliances and cause wars; it also impacted the diplomacy, military, economy, politics, culture, and society of the superpowers and dozens of other nations. In the United States, the fear of communism led numerous states to require their public employees, including teachers, to take loyalty oaths. President Dwight D. Eisenhower, a committed Cold Warrior, nonetheless used his Farewell Address to warn his fellow citizens that a growing "military-industrial complex" and dependency on the federal government for scientific and technological innovation (both results of the Cold War) threatened self-government and individual liberty (Document 19).

The costs of the Cold War were enormous; so, too, its hazards. The United States spent trillions of dollars to advance its Cold War policies and programs. Just one of the proxy wars, the Korean War (Documents 8-9), took the lives of more than 1.2 million combatants (including 36,574 Americans), yet the three-year war ended precisely where it started, with a communist regime north of the 38th parallel on the Korean peninsula. In Southeast Asia, the United States committed itself to an unsuccessful war to prevent the unification of Vietnam under communism (Documents 21, 29-31, 34). The difficulties of forcing Vietnam's civil conflict to fit the policy of containment raised concerns within the government (Document 32) and led some Americans, including President Jimmy Carter, to ask if the United States had undermined its own principles in fighting this war (Documents 33 and 40). Finally, the arsenals of nuclear weapons amassed by the United States and the Soviet Union (as well as other nations) held the power to kill a majority of the world's population and likely destroy the planet's ability to sustain life. The 1962 Cuban Missile Crisis, a showdown between the United States and the Soviet Union, almost triggered a nuclear war (Documents 23-26).

Acutely aware of the ultimate danger of the Cold War, Soviet and American leaders often worked to ease tensions. In 1959, the United States hosted an exhibit in Moscow on American society and industry. Soviet leader Nikita Khrushchev accompanied Vice President Richard Nixon on a tour of the exhibit, leading to a spirited but friendly exchange between the two men about the merits and flaws of communism, capitalism, and democracy. Both leaders stood their ground during the Kitchen Debate (so-called because one back-and-forth took place in a model of an American kitchen), but they also agreed that mutual understanding inhibited conflict (Document 18). In 1963, the United States and the Soviet Union, along with other nations, drafted and signed a nuclear test ban treaty in hopes that the quest for more powerful nuclear arms could be slowed (Document 28). In 1972, Nixon, now president, visited communist China as part of a strategy known as détente, a French word that in this context means an easing of tensions (Document 36). The historic meeting enabled the United States and China to soon restore diplomatic and trade relations.

However, the entrenched differences between the United States and the Soviet Union and their respective allies meant that crises could erupt at any time. In 1976, U.S. national security policymakers discussed various ways, including military action, to disrupt the foreign policy of communist Cuba, but they also noted the danger of such actions provoking the Soviet Union (Document 39). In 1979, the Soviet invasion of Afghanistan incurred a strong response from the United States (Document 41). The era of détente abruptly ended.

During the 1980s, President Ronald Reagan was determined to bring the Cold War to a peaceful end. Though critics charged that he was intensifying the Cold War by committing the United States to a massive military buildup, Reagan countered that a strengthened defense, including an experimental anti-missile program known as the Strategic Defense Initiative, advanced peace by deterring communist aggression (Document 42). Reagan also drafted nuclear arms reduction agreements with the Soviet Union. As the president made clear in a 1987 speech, the ultimate goal of the United States and its allies was not simply to manage the Cold War – it was to peacefully advance freedom and democracy, sweeping communism aside in the process (Document 43). By the late 1980s, democratic movements in Poland and Czechoslovakia, both communist nations, hinted that the Cold War might well be at a turning point.

Indeed, aware that drastic changes were needed to save communism, Soviet leader Mikhail Gorbachev undertook major internal reforms and, just as important, significantly changed the terms of Soviet control of Eastern Europe's communist states. In 1956, the Soviet Union had crushed a democratic uprising in communist Hungary (Document 17); thirty years later, Gorbachev announced that the Soviet Union would not use force to intervene in the domestic affairs of communist nations. In 1989, Gorbachev spoke hopefully of Europe as a "common home" in which communist nations worked peacefully with democratic countries to solve mutual problems. U.S. intelligence analysts cautioned that the Soviet Union remained a threat (Document 44), yet communism was faltering and falling. Later that year, the Berlin Wall – the most visible sign of the division between the communist and free worlds in Europe (Documents 27 and 43) – came down, and the joyous meeting of Berliners on this previously heavily guarded border signified the end of the Cold War (Document 45).

The purpose of this collection is to provide teachers with a selection of primary sources that document the multi-faceted Cold War. A variety of sources are used to represent, as much as possible, the conflict's most significant developments and patterns. The addresses and statements of Cold War-era presidents offer insight into the principles and purposes of U.S. policies. Congressional resolutions and testimony before Congress show the key role of the legislative branch. Declassified documents from the National Security Agency, Department of State, and National Security Council offer a glimpse into the planning of covert operations, management of international propaganda, and Soviet espionage in the United States, among other topics. Although a majority of the sources relate to the diplomatic, military, and political sides of the Cold War, select documents provide perspective on the conflict's effects on American society. The sources are presented in chronological order, but a thematic table of contents is also provided (Appendix A), so that users may quickly find documents of interest.

Acknowledgments

Several people assisted me in the preparation of this collection, and I'm grateful for their contributions. Eric Pullin and John Moser provided excellent suggestions on the selection of documents. Ali Brosky ably converted and formatted documents for me. Series editor David Tucker offered expert guidance and editing and had immediate answers for all my questions.

The Cold War:
Core Documents

Document 1

The Long Telegram
George Kennan
February 22, 1946

U.S. diplomat, scholar, and public intellectual George Kennan (1904 – 2005) was one of the nation's most perceptive observers of the Soviet Union during the early Cold War. Kennan entered the Foreign Service in 1926. Fluent in Russian, he was stationed in Latvia prior to the U.S. diplomatic recognition of the Soviet Union in 1933. He served on the embassy staff in Moscow before and after World War II.

In February 1946, Kennan authored a lengthy analysis commonly called the Long Telegram. (To cable a message more than 5,000 words long from Moscow to Washington was highly unusual, showing the urgency of the report). Kennan had been asked to explain why the Soviet Union was opposed to the newly formed World Bank and International Monetary Fund, but he also took the opportunity to offer a perceptive, wide-ranging essay about the methods and motives of Soviet communism and how the United States should respond. This was the policy of containment, which Kennan described in detail in an article entitled "The Sources of Soviet Conduct," published in Foreign Affairs *in 1947. Its essence, as Kennan phrased it in that article, was that "the main element of any United States policy toward the Soviet Union must be that of a long-term, patient but firm and vigilant containment of Russian expansive tendencies."*

Containment became the keystone of America's Cold War policies. Secretary of State George Marshall appointed Kennan the first director of the State Department's Policy Planning Staff, a position he held from 1947 – 1948. However, the diplomat's finer points were soon forgotten. The Truman Doctrine (Document 2) all but promised that the United States would resist each and every instance of Soviet expansion. Kennan had advised that the United States must carefully choose its points of resistance, based upon a dispassionate measure of the nation's long-term global aims. While Kennan had explained that containment could take many forms, by 1950 containment had been militarized by NSC 68 (Document 6). A close reading and comparison of these three documents – the Long Telegram, the Truman Doctrine, and NSC 68 – is an excellent way to trace the creation and rapid evolution of containment.

Source: The Chargé in the Soviet Union (Kennan) to the Secretary of State, February 22, 1946 [Document 475], The Foreign Relations of the United States,

1946, Vol. VI, Eastern Europe, the Soviet Union (*Washington, D.C.: U.S. Department of State, Office of the Historian, 1969*).

Answer to Dept's 284, Feb 3 [telegram][1] involves questions so intricate, so delicate, so strange to our form of thought, and so important to analysis of our international environment that I cannot compress answers into single brief message without yielding to what I feel would be dangerous degree of over-simplification. I hope, therefore, Dept will bear with me if I submit in answer to this question five parts, subjects of which will be roughly as follows:

(1) Basic features of post-war Soviet outlook.
(2) Background of this outlook.
(3) Its projection in practical policy on official level.
(4) Its projection on unofficial level.
(5) Practical deductions from standpoint of US policy.

I apologize in advance for this burdening of telegraphic channel; but questions involved are of such urgent importance, particularly in view of recent events, that our answers to them, if they deserve attention at all, seem to me to deserve it at once. There follows

Part 1: Basic Features of Post War Soviet Outlook, as Put Forward by Official Propaganda Machine, Are as Follows:

(a) USSR still lives in antagonistic "capitalist encirclement" with which in the long run there can be no permanent peaceful coexistence. As stated by Stalin in 1927 to a delegation of American workers:

"In course of further development of international revolution there will emerge two centers of world significance: a socialist center, drawing to itself the countries which tend toward socialism, and a capitalist center, drawing to itself the countries that incline toward capitalism. Battle between these two centers for command of world economy will decide fate of capitalism and of communism in entire world."

(b) Capitalist world is beset with internal conflicts, inherent in nature of capitalist society. These conflicts are insoluble by means of peaceful compromise. Greatest of them is that between England and US.

(c) Internal conflicts of capitalism inevitably generate wars. Wars thus generated may be of two kinds: intra-capitalist wars between two capitalist states, and wars of intervention against socialist world. Smart capitalists, vainly

---

[1] Here Kennan refers to the request from the State Department for his analysis.

seeking escape from inner conflicts of capitalism, incline toward latter [that is, wars against socialist nations] ...

So much for premises. To what deductions do they lead from standpoint of Soviet policy? To following:

(a) Everything must be done to advance relative strength of USSR as factor in international society. Conversely, no opportunity must be missed to reduce strength and influence, collectively as well as individually, of capitalist powers.

(b) Soviet efforts, and those of Russia's friends abroad, must be directed toward deepening and exploiting of differences and conflicts between capitalist powers. If these eventually deepen into an "imperialist" war, this war must be turned into revolutionary upheavals within the various capitalist countries.

(c) "Democratic-progressive" elements abroad are to be utilized to maximum to bring pressure to bear on capitalist governments along lines agreeable to Soviet interests ...

Part 2: Background of Outlook

Before examining ramifications of this party line in practice there are certain aspects of it to which I wish to draw attention.

First, it does not represent natural outlook of Russian people. [Russians] are, by and large, friendly to outside world, eager for experience of it, eager to measure against it talents they are conscious of possessing, eager above all to live in peace and enjoy fruits of their own labor. Party line only represents thesis which official propaganda machine puts forward with great skill and persistence to a public often remarkably resistant in the stronghold of its innermost thoughts. But party line is binding for outlook and conduct of people who make up apparatus of power – party, secret police and Government – and it is exclusively with these that we have to deal.

Second, please note that premises on which this party line is based are for most part simply not true. Experience has shown that peaceful and mutually profitable coexistence of capitalist and socialist states is entirely possible. . . . At bottom of Kremlin's[2] neurotic view of world affairs is traditional and instinctive Russian sense of insecurity . . . they have always feared foreign penetration, feared direct contact between Western world and their own, feared what would happen if Russians learned truth about world without or if foreigners learned truth about world within. And they have learned to seek security only in patient but deadly struggle for total destruction of rival power, never in compacts and compromises with it.

---

[2] The Kremlin was the seat of government power in the Soviet capital of Moscow. The reference is similar to using "Washington" as a term for the U.S. government.

It was no coincidence that Marxism [*that is, communism*], which had smoldered ineffectively for half a century in Western Europe, caught hold and blazed for first time in Russia [*where*] ... in the name of Marxism they sacrificed every single ethical value in their methods and tactics. Today they cannot dispense with it. It is fig leaf of their moral and intellectual respectability. Without it they would stand before history, at best, as only the last of that long succession of cruel and wasteful Russian rulers who have relentlessly forced country on to ever new heights of military power in order to guarantee external security of their internally weak regimes ...

Part 3: Projection of Soviet Outlook in Practical Policy on Official Level

We have now seen nature and background of Soviet program. What may we expect by way of its practical implementation? ...

(a) Internal policy devoted to increasing in every way strength and prestige of Soviet state: intensive military-industrialization; maximum development of armed forces; great displays to impress outsiders; continued secretiveness about internal matters, designed to conceal weaknesses and to keep opponents in dark.

(b) Wherever it is considered timely and promising, efforts will be made to advance official limits of Soviet power. For the moment, these efforts are restricted to certain neighboring points conceived of here as being of immediate strategic necessity, such as Northern Iran, Turkey ...

(e) Russians will strive energetically to develop Soviet representation in, and official ties with, countries in which they sense strong possibilities of opposition to Western centers of power. This applies to such widely separated points as Germany, Argentina, Middle Eastern countries, etc. ...

Part 4: Following May Be Said as to What We May Expect by Way of Implementation of Basic Soviet Policies on Unofficial, or Subterranean Plane ... for Which Soviet Government Accepts no Responsibility ...

(a) To undermine general political and strategic potential of major western powers. Efforts will be made in such countries to disrupt national self confidence, to hamstring measures of national defense, to increase social and industrial unrest, to stimulate all forms of disunity. All persons with grievances, whether economic or racial, will be urged to seek redress not in mediation and compromise, but in defiant violent struggle for destruction of other elements of society. Here poor will be set against rich, black against white, young against old, newcomers against established residents, etc.

(b) On unofficial plane particularly violent efforts will be made to weaken power and influence of Western Powers [on] colonial backward, or dependent peoples. On this level, no holds will be barred. Mistakes and weaknesses of western colonial administration will be mercilessly exposed and exploited. Liberal opinion in Western countries will be mobilized to weaken colonial policies. Resentment among dependent peoples will be stimulated . . .

(c) Where individual governments stand in path of Soviet purposes pressure will be brought for their removal from office. This can happen where governments directly oppose Soviet foreign policy aims (Turkey, Iran), where they seal their territories off against Communist penetration (Switzerland, Portugal), or where they compete too strongly . . .

(d) In foreign countries Communists will, as a rule, work toward destruction of all forms of personal independence, economic, political or moral . . .

(e) Everything possible will be done to set major Western Powers against each other . . .

(f) In general, all Soviet efforts on unofficial international plane will be negative and destructive in character, designed to tear down sources of strength beyond reach of Soviet control. This is only in line with basic Soviet instinct that there can be no compromise with rival power and that constructive work can start only when communist power is dominant . . .

Part 5: [Practical Deductions From Standpoint of US Policy]

In summary, we have here a political force committed fanatically to the belief that with US there can be no permanent *modus vivendi*,[3] that it is desirable and necessary that the internal harmony of our society be disrupted, our traditional way of life be destroyed, the international authority of our state be broken, if Soviet power is to be secure. This political force has complete power of disposition over energies of one of world's greatest peoples and resources of world's richest national territory, and is borne along by deep and powerful currents of Russian nationalism . . . this is admittedly not a pleasant picture . . . but I would like to record my conviction that problem is within our power to solve – and that without recourse to any general military conflict. And in support of this conviction there are certain observations of a more encouraging nature I should like to make:

(1) Soviet power, unlike that of Hitlerite Germany, is neither schematic nor adventuristic. It does not work by fixed plans. It does not take unnecessary risks. Impervious to logic of reason, and it is highly sensitive to logic of force. For this reason it can easily withdraw – and usually does when strong resistance is encountered at any point. Thus, if the adversary has sufficient force and makes

---

[3] Way to live together or co-exist.

clear his readiness to use it, he rarely has to do so. If situations are properly handled there need be no prestige-engaging showdowns.

(2) Gauged against Western World as a whole, Soviets are still by far the weaker force. Thus, their success will really depend on degree of cohesion, firmness and vigor which Western World can muster. And this is factor which it is within our power to influence.

(3) Success of Soviet system, as form of internal power, is not yet finally proven. It has yet to be demonstrated that it can survive supreme test of successive transfer of power from one individual or group to another ...

(4) All Soviet propaganda beyond Soviet security sphere is basically negative and destructive. It should therefore be relatively easy to combat it by any intelligent and really constructive program.

For those reasons I think we may approach calmly and with good heart problem of how to deal with Russia. As to how this approach should be made, I only wish to advance, by way of conclusion, following comments:

(1) Our first step must be to apprehend, and recognize for what it is, the nature of the movement with which we are dealing. We must study it with same courage, detachment, objectivity, and same determination not to be emotionally provoked or unseated by it ...

(2) We must see that our public is educated to realities of Russian situation. I cannot over-emphasize importance of this. Press cannot do this alone. It must be done mainly by Government, which is necessarily more experienced and better informed on practical problems involved ... I am convinced that there would be far less hysterical anti-Sovietism in our country today if realities of this situation were better understood by our people ...

(3) Much depends on health and vigor of our own society. World communism is like malignant parasite which feeds only on diseased tissue. This is point at which domestic and foreign policies meet. Every courageous and incisive measure to solve internal problems of our own society, to improve self-confidence, discipline, morale and community spirit of our own people, is a diplomatic victory over Moscow ...

(4) We must formulate and put forward for other nations a much more positive and constructive picture of sort of world we would like to see than we have put forward in past. It is not enough to urge people to develop political processes similar to our own. Many foreign peoples, in Europe at least, are tired and frightened by experiences of past, and are less interested in abstract freedom than in security. They are seeking guidance rather than responsibilities. We should be better able than Russians to give them this. And unless we do, Russians certainly will.

(5) Finally we must have courage and self-confidence to cling to our own methods and conceptions of human society. After all, the greatest danger that can befall us in coping with this problem of Soviet communism, is that we shall allow ourselves to become like those with whom we are coping.

Document 2

Special Message to the Congress on Greece and Turkey (The Truman Doctrine)

President Harry S. Truman
March 12, 1947

In this speech, Democratic President Harry S. Truman hoped to persuade Congress to provide $400 million in economic and military aid to Greece and Turkey. Both nations, especially Greece, had emerged from World War II in difficult situations. The German occupation of Greece resulted in widespread damage to the impoverished nation's infrastructure and economy. Civil conflict in Greece threatened to topple its government, and communist rebels in Greece received support from the communist states of Bulgaria and Yugoslavia. Though Turkey was spared wartime devastation, after the war the Soviet Union began pressuring the Turkish government to allow the Soviets to set up military bases in the Black Sea Straits. In February 1947, the British government, which had been financially assisting Greece, informed the United States that it could no longer afford this aid.

These developments caused great alarm within the U.S. State Department. Should the Soviet Union gain control of the Black Sea Straits, it would have unchecked access to the Mediterranean Sea. Communist influence in Greece would likewise increase Soviet power in an area of vital importance to the United States and its European allies. George Kennan's prediction that the Soviet Union would slowly but steadily undermine governments in areas where it wanted to expand appeared to be coming true (Document 1).

Prior to his speech, Truman met with leaders of Congress, now controlled by the opposition party. (Republicans had won a commanding majority during the 1946 midterm elections.) Senator Arthur Vandenberg (R-Mich.), chair of the Senate Foreign Relations Committee, purportedly told the president that he would need to "scare" the American people in order to persuade them to assist Greece and Turkey. Whether or not Vandenberg actually offered such advice, Truman provided a somber view of the present world situation. After detailing the economic and political struggles of Greece and Turkey, the president reminded listeners of the principles for which the United States fought in World War II, especially the right of all people to determine the form of government under which they live. (For examples, see World War II: Core Documents, Documents 5 and 10). To ignore Greece and Turkey in their time of need, Truman suggested, would betray the hard-won Allied victory and contribute to global instability by allowing communism to spread.

The influence of the speech was tremendous. After lengthy debate, Congress approved the aid request. Greece received most of the aid, $300 million, with the remainder, $100 million, going to Turkey. Both nations became U.S. allies; both joined the North Atlantic Treaty Organization organized by the United States two years later (1949). The greatest result of the speech was the so-called doctrine it established. In the heart of the speech, Truman outlined two ways of life. The first, based upon "the will of the majority," provides citizens with basic rights and freedoms – a constitutional democracy, in other words. The second way of life, carried out by "the will of a minority," is forced upon people by "terror and oppression." Although the president only referred to communism once and never mentioned the Soviet Union by name in his address, the association was clear: the United States supports and defends the first way of life while the Soviet Union aggressively advances the second. Therefore, the president asserted, "It must be the policy of the United States to support free peoples who are resisting attempted subjugation by armed minorities or by outside pressures." This statement helped establish the containment of communism as the basic goal of U.S. foreign policy during the Cold War. The influence of the Truman Doctrine is evident in numerous documents in this collection, including the Marshall Plan (Document 3), NSC 68 (Document 6), Truman's Farewell Address (Document 14), John F. Kennedy's Inaugural Address (Document 20), and the Rusk-McNamara Report (Document 21).

Source: Address of the President of the United States, Recommendation for Assistance to Greece and Turkey, March 12, 1947. Available at https://goo.gl/AjyAtq.

The gravity of the situation which confronts the world today necessitates my appearance before a joint session of the Congress. The foreign policy and the national security of this country are involved.

One aspect of the present situation, which I wish to present to you at this time for your consideration and decision, concerns Greece and Turkey.

The United States has received from the Greek Government an urgent appeal for financial and economic assistance . . . if Greece is to survive as a free nation.

I do not believe that the American people and the Congress wish to turn a deaf ear to the appeal of the Greek Government. . . .

Greece is today without funds to finance the importation of those goods which are essential to bare subsistence. Under these circumstances the people of Greece cannot make progress in solving their problems of reconstruction. Greece is in desperate need of financial and economic assistance to enable it to resume purchases of food, clothing, fuel, and seeds. These are indispensable for the subsistence of its people and are obtainable only from abroad. Greece must have help to import the goods necessary to restore internal order and security so essential for economic and political recovery. . . .

The very existence of the Greek state is today threatened by the terrorist activities of several thousand armed men, led by Communists, who defy the Government's authority at a number of points . . . .

[T]he Greek Government is unable to cope with the situation. The Greek Army is small and poorly equipped. It needs supplies and equipment if it is to restore the authority of the Government throughout Greek territory.

Greece must have assistance if it is to become a self-supporting and self-respecting democracy.

The United States must supply that assistance. We have already extended to Greece certain types of relief and economic aid, but these are inadequate.

There is no other country to which democratic Greece can turn. . . .

We have considered how the United Nations might assist in this crisis. But the situation is an urgent one requiring immediate action, and the United Nations and its related organizations are not in a position to extend help of the kind that is required.

It is important to note that the Greek Government has asked for our aid in utilizing effectively the financial and other assistance we may give to Greece, and in improving public administration. It is of the utmost importance that we supervise the use of any funds made available to Greece, in such a manner that each dollar spent will count toward making Greece self-supporting, and will help to build an economy in which a healthy democracy can flourish.

No government is perfect. One of the chief virtues of a democracy, however, is that its defects are always visible and under democratic processes can be pointed out and corrected. The Government of Greece is not perfect. Nevertheless it represents 85 per cent of the members of the Greek parliament who were chosen in an election last year. . . .

Greece's neighbor, Turkey, also deserves our attention.

The future of Turkey as an independent and economically sound state is clearly no less important to the freedom-loving peoples of the world than the future of Greece. The circumstances in which Turkey finds itself today are considerably different from those of Greece. Turkey has been spared the disasters that have beset Greece; and during the war,[1] the United States and

---

[1] World War II.

Great Britain furnished Turkey with material aid. Nevertheless, Turkey now needs our support. . . .

I am fully aware of the broad implications involved if the United States extends assistance to Greece and Turkey, and I shall discuss these implications with you at this time.

One of the primary objectives of the foreign policy of the United States is the creation of conditions in which we and other nations will be able to work out a way of life free from coercion. This was a fundamental issue in the war with Germany and Japan. Our victory was won over countries which sought to impose their will, and their way of life, upon other nations.

To insure the peaceful development of nations, free from coercion, the United States has taken a leading part in establishing the United Nations. The United Nations is designed to make possible lasting freedom and independence for all its members. We shall not realize our objectives, however, unless we are willing to help free people to maintain their free institutions and their national integrity against aggressive movements that seek to impose upon them totalitarian regimes. . . .

At the present moment in world history nearly every nation must choose between alternative ways of life. The choice is too often not a free one.

One way of life is based upon the will of the majority, and is distinguished by free institutions, representative government, free elections, guaranties of individual liberty, freedom of speech and religion, and freedom from political oppression.

The second way of life is based upon the will of a minority forcibly imposed upon the majority. It relies upon terror and oppression, a controlled press and radio, fixed elections, and the suppression of personal freedoms.

I believe that it must be the policy of the United States to support free peoples who are resisting attempted subjugation by armed minorities or by outside pressures.

I believe that we must assist free peoples to work out their own destinies in their own way.

I believe that our help should be primarily through economic and financial aid which is essential to economic stability and orderly political processes. . . .

Should we fail to aid Greece and Turkey in this fateful hour, the effect will be far-reaching to the West as well as to the East.

We must take immediate and resolute action.

I, therefore, ask the Congress to provide authority for assistance to Greece and Turkey in the amount of $400,000,000. . . .

In addition to funds, I ask the Congress to authorize the detail of American civilian and military personnel to Greece and Turkey, at the request of those countries, to assist in the tasks of reconstruction. . . .

The United States contributed $341,000,000,000 toward winning World War II. This is an investment in world freedom and world peace.

The assistance that I am recommending for Greece and Turkey amounts to little more than one-tenth of 1 per cent of this investment. It is only common sense that we should safeguard this investment and make sure that it was not in vain.

The seeds of totalitarian regimes are nurtured by misery and want. They spread and grow in the evil soil of poverty and strife. They reach their full growth when the hope of a people for a better life has died.

We must keep that hope alive.

The free peoples of the world look to us for support in maintaining their freedoms.

If we falter in our leadership, we may endanger the peace of the world – and we shall surely endanger the welfare of our own nation.

Great responsibilities have been placed upon us by the swift movement of events.

I am confident that the Congress will face these responsibilities squarely.

Document 3

"European Initiative Essential to Economic Recovery" (The Marshall Plan)

George C. Marshall

June 5, 1947

World War II had ended in Europe almost two years before George Marshall, then serving as Secretary of State, delivered this speech at Harvard University's 1947 commencement ceremony, but the devastation of the war had not yet been overcome. As Marshall – who had served as the U.S. Army Chief of Staff during the war – observed, complete recovery required the assistance of the United States.

The United States had several motives to make such an offer of assistance. As President Truman had argued in his March 1947 speech requesting aid for Greece and Turkey (Document 2), the United States could not allow postwar political and economic upheaval to obstruct the creation or security of democratic governments. Marshall implied that continued chaos and deprivation in Europe might lead desperate populations to embrace radical (read: communist) ideologies. The Marshall Plan, as it was informally called, therefore advanced the policy of containment by trying to stop the spread of communism while nurturing democracy and capitalism. Marshall and other U.S. policymakers also worried about the possibility of a postwar depression – sending American manufactured goods to European markets could prevent such an economic collapse. Finally, the United States hoped to encourage the integration of the Western European economy across borders. Such integration was not only good for international trade, it also diminished the likelihood of future European conflict.

The Soviet Union refused to allow its communist satellite states to participate in the Marshall Plan, a move that the United States had anticipated and hoped for, since a primary purpose of the aid was to promote democracy and capitalism. Congressional debate on the aid was protracted and heated, with approval delayed until the spring of 1948. (The fall of the Czech government to communism in February 1948 helped clinch passage.) Officially known as the European Recovery Program, the plan cost $13.3 billion over its three-year duration (1948 – 1951). The United States did not extend loans or offer cash grants to the recipients, which included, among many other nations, France, Great Britain, West Germany, and Italy. Instead, the United States sent American-made goods or resources (vehicles, factory equipment, agricultural machinery, and petroleum) to the participating countries based on their needs; in return, these nations paid currency into an account that funded infrastructure projects in the program zone.

Although the Marshall Plan did not achieve its aim of fully integrating the Western European economy, it strengthened the Western alliance, brought West Germany into that alliance, enabled substantial economic recovery, and hardened the Iron Curtain between West and East.

Source: George C. Marshall, "European Initiative Essential to Economic Recovery," June 5, 1947. Available at https://goo.gl/u48dWH.

———————————————————

I need not tell you gentlemen that the world situation is very serious. That must be apparent to all intelligent people. I think one difficulty is that the problem is one of such enormous complexity that the very mass of facts presented to the public by press and radio make it exceedingly difficult for the man in the street to reach a clear appraisement of the situation. Furthermore, the people of this country are distant from the troubled areas of the earth and it is hard for them to comprehend the plight and consequent reaction of the long-suffering peoples, and the effect of those reactions on their governments in connection with our efforts to promote peace in the world.

In considering the requirements for the rehabilitation of Europe, the physical loss of life, the visible destruction of cities, factories, mines, and railroads was correctly estimated, but it has become obvious during recent months that this visible destruction was probably less serious than the dislocation of the entire fabric of European economy. For the past 10 years conditions have been highly abnormal. The feverish preparation for war and the more feverish maintenance of the war effort engulfed all aspects of national economies. Machinery has fallen into disrepair or is entirely obsolete. Under the arbitrary and destructive Nazi rule, virtually every possible enterprise was geared into the German war machine. Long-standing commercial ties, private institutions, banks, insurance companies, and shipping companies disappeared, through loss of capital, absorption through nationalization, or by simple destruction. In many countries, confidence in the local currency has been severely shaken. The breakdown of the business structure of Europe during the war was complete. Recovery has been seriously retarded by the fact that two years after the close of hostilities a peace settlement with Germany and Austria has not been agreed upon. But even given a more prompt solution of these difficult problems, the rehabilitation of the economic structure of Europe quite evidently will require a much longer time and greater effort than had been foreseen.

There is a phase of this matter which is both interesting and serious. The farmer has always produced the foodstuffs to exchange with the city dweller for the other necessities of life. This division of labor is the basis of modern civilization. At the present time it is threatened with breakdown. The town and city industries are not producing adequate goods to exchange with the food-producing farmer. Raw materials and fuel are in short supply. Machinery is lacking or worn out. The farmer or the peasant cannot find the goods for sale which he desires to purchase. So the sale of his farm produce for money which he cannot use seems to him an unprofitable transaction. He, therefore, has withdrawn many fields from crop cultivation and is using them for grazing. He feeds more grain to stock and finds for himself and his family an ample supply of food, however short he may be on clothing and the other ordinary gadgets of civilization. Meanwhile people in the cities are short of food and fuel. So the governments are forced to use their foreign money and credits to procure these necessities abroad. This process exhausts funds which are urgently needed for reconstruction. Thus a very serious situation is rapidly developing which bodes no good for the world. The modern system of the division of labor upon which the exchange of products is based is in danger of breaking down.

The truth of the matter is that Europe's requirements for the next three or four years of foreign food and other essential products – principally from America – are so much greater than her present ability to pay that she must have substantial additional help or face economic, social, and political deterioration of a very grave character.

The remedy lies in breaking the vicious circle and restoring the confidence of the European people in the economic future of their own countries and of Europe as a whole. The manufacturer and the farmer throughout wide areas must be able and willing to exchange their products for currencies the continuing value of which is not open to question.

Aside from the demoralizing effect on the world at large and the possibilities of disturbances arising as a result of the desperation of the people concerned, the consequences to the economy of the United States should be apparent to all. It is logical that the United States should do whatever it is able to do to assist in the return of normal economic health in the world, without which there can be no political stability and no assured peace. Our policy is directed not against any country or doctrine but against hunger, poverty, desperation, and chaos. Its purpose should be the revival of working economy in the world so as to permit the emergence of political and social conditions in which free institutions can exist. Such assistance, I am convinced, must not be on a piecemeal basis as various crises develop. Any assistance that this Government may render in the future should provide a cure rather than a mere palliative. Any government that is willing to assist in the task of recovery will find full cooperation, I am sure, on the part of the United States Government. Any government which maneuvers to block the recovery of other countries cannot expect help from us. Furthermore, governments, political parties, or groups which seek to perpetuate human misery in order to profit therefrom politically or otherwise will encounter the opposition of the United States.

It is already evident that, before the United States Government can proceed much further in its efforts to alleviate the situation and help start the European world on its way to recovery, there must be some agreement among the countries of Europe as to the requirements of the situation and the part those countries themselves will take in order to give proper effect to whatever action might be undertaken by this Government. It would be neither fitting nor efficacious for this Government to undertake to draw up unilaterally a program designed to place Europe on its feet economically. This is the business of the Europeans. The initiative, I think, must come from Europe. The role of this country should consist of friendly aid in the drafting of a European program so far as it may be practical for us to do so. The program should be a joint one, agreed to by a number, if not all, European nations.

An essential part of any successful action on the part of the United States is an understanding on the part of the people of America of the character of the problem and the remedies to be applied. Political passion and prejudice should have no part. With foresight, and a willingness on the part of our people to face up to the vast responsibilities which history has clearly placed upon our country, the difficulties I have outlined can and will be overcome.

Document 4

"Crisis in Asia – An Examination of U.S. Policy"
Dean Acheson
January 12, 1950

By the time Secretary of State Dean Acheson delivered this speech to the National Press Club in Washington, D.C., the Truman administration (1945 – 1953) had weathered considerable criticism from Congressional Republicans for the outcome of the Chinese Civil War, which put a communist regime into power in late 1949. In the view of many conservatives, the administration was partially responsible for the communist takeover of China because it had failed to adequately support the Chinese nationalists, led by Chiang Kai-shek, who had battled Mao Tse-Tung's communists for years. (Accusations by Senator Joseph McCarthy [R-Wisc.] that communists within the State Department had sabotaged America's China policy attracted national attention in February 1950; Document 5.) For their part, Truman's policymakers documented the many failings of the nationalists, including corruption and the misuse of U.S. money and equipment, in order to justify the decision to cut off American support.

The main purpose of Acheson's speech was to outline the strategic priorities of the United States in East Asia. In doing so, Acheson drew a line that extended from the Aleutian Islands to Japan, then to the Ryukyu Islands (a string of islands that stretches from Japan southwest toward Taiwan) and the Philippines (which had obtained independence from the United States three years prior). The United States would not assume sole responsibility for providing military assistance elsewhere in the region. In June, the North Korean invasion of South Korea prompted accusations that Acheson's speech had emboldened the communists to invade because the United States had drawn a line that bypassed the Korean peninsula. However, Kim Il Sung, the communist dictator of North Korea, was hardly waiting for cues from the U.S. Secretary of State to carry out an attack he had been long plotting. The invasion did draw the United States into war, but on the terms suggested by Acheson in this speech: through the United Nations, of which the Republic of Korea was a member (Documents 8-9).

Source: "Crisis in Asia: An Examination of U.S. Policy," Department of State Bulletin, Vol. XXII, no. 551 (January 23, 1950), 111-18.

... I am frequently asked: Has the State Department got an Asian policy? And it seems to me that that discloses such a depth of ignorance that it is very hard to begin to deal with it. The peoples of Asia are so incredibly diverse and their problems are so incredibly diverse that how could anyone ... believe that he had a uniform policy which would deal with all of them. On the other hand, there are very important similarities in ideas and in problems among the peoples of Asia and so what we come to, after we understand these diversities and these common attitudes of mind, is the fact that there must be certain similarities of approach, ...

... There is in this vast area [*Asia*] what we might call a developing Asian consciousness, and a developing pattern, and this, I think, is based upon two factors ...

One of these factors is a revulsion against the acceptance of misery and poverty as the normal condition of life. Throughout all of this vast area, you have that fundamental revolutionary aspect in mind and belief. The other common aspect that they have is the revulsion against foreign domination. Whether that foreign domination takes the form of colonialism or whether it takes the form of imperialism, they are through with it. They have had enough of it, and they want no more. ...

Now, may I suggest to you that much of the bewilderment which has seized the minds of many of us about recent developments in China[1] comes from a failure to understand this basic revolutionary force which is loose in Asia. The reasons for the fall of the Nationalist Government[2] in China are preoccupying many people. All sorts of reasons have been attributed to it. Most commonly, it is said in various speeches and publications that it is the result of American bungling, that we are incompetent, that we did not understand, that American aid was too little, that we did the wrong things at the wrong time. ...

... Now, what I ask you to do is to stop looking for a moment under the bed and under the chair and under the rug to find out these reasons, but rather to look at the broad picture and see whether something doesn't suggest itself.
...

... What has happened in my judgment is that the almost inexhaustible patience of the Chinese people in their misery ended. They did not bother to overthrow this government. There was really nothing to overthrow. They simply ignored it .... They completely withdrew their support from this government, and when that support was withdrawn, the whole military

---

[1] The rise to power of the Chinese communists and the creation of the People's Republic of China, a communist state.

[2] The Chinese Nationalists, led by Chiang Kai-shek, had fought the Chinese communists during China's long civil war.

establishment disintegrated. Added to the grossest incompetence ever experienced by any military command was this total lack of support both in the armies and in the country, and so the whole matter just simply disintegrated.

The Communists did not create this. The Communists did not create this condition. They did not create this revolutionary spirit. They did not create a great force which moved out from under Chiang Kai-shek. But they were shrewd and cunning to mount it, to ride this thing into victory and into power. . . .

Now, let me come to another underlying and important factor which determines our relations and, in turn, our policy with the peoples of Asia. That is the attitude of the Soviet Union toward Asia, and particularly towards those parts of Asia which are contiguous to the Soviet Union, and with great particularity this afternoon, to north China.

The attitude and interest of the Russians in north China, and in these other areas as well, long antedates communism. This is not something that has come out of communism at all. It long antedates it. But the Communist regime has added new methods, new skills, and new concepts to the thrust of Russian imperialism. . . . [W]hat is happening in China is that the Soviet Union is detaching the northern provinces of China from China and is attaching them to the Soviet Union. . . .

What does that mean for us? It means something very, very significant. It means that nothing that we do and nothing that we say must be allowed to obscure the reality of this fact. All the efforts of propaganda will not be able to obscure it. The only thing that can obscure it is the folly of ill-conceived adventures on our part which easily could do so, and I urge all who are thinking about these foolish adventures to remember that we must not seize the unenviable position which the Russians have carved out for themselves. . . . We must take the position we have always taken – that anyone who violates the integrity of China is the enemy of China and is acting contrary to our own interest. That, I suggest to you this afternoon, is the first and the greatest rule in regard to the formulation of American policy toward Asia.

I suggest that the second rule is very like the first. That is to keep our own purposes perfectly straight, perfectly pure, . . .

What is the situation in regard to the military security of the Pacific area, and what is our policy in regard to it?

In the first place, the defeat and the disarmament of Japan has placed upon the United States the necessity of assuming the military defense of Japan so long as that is required, both in the interest of our security and in the interests of the security of the entire Pacific area and, in all honor, in the interest of Japanese security. We have American – and there are Australian – troops in Japan. I am not in a position to speak for the Australians, but I can assure you that there is no intention of any sort of abandoning or weakening the defenses of Japan and that whatever arrangements are to be made either through permanent settlement or otherwise, that defense must and shall be maintained.

The defensive perimeter runs along the Aleutians to Japan and then goes to the Ryukyus. We hold important defense positions in the Ryukyu Islands[3], and those we will continue to hold. In the interest of the population of the Ryukyu Islands, we will at an appropriate time offer to hold these islands under trusteeship of the United Nations. But they are essential parts of the defensive perimeter of the Pacific, and they must and will be held.

The defensive perimeter runs from the Ryukyus to the Philippine Islands. Our relations, our defensive relations with the Philippines are contained in agreements between us. Those agreements are being loyally carried out and will be loyally carried out. Both peoples have learned by bitter experience the vital connections between our mutual defense requirements. We are in no doubt about that, and it is hardly necessary for me to say an attack on the Philippines could not and would not be tolerated by the United States. But I hasten to add that no one perceives the imminence of any such attack.

So far as the military security of other areas in the Pacific is concerned, it must be clear that no person can guarantee these areas against military attack. But it must also be clear that such a guarantee is hardly sensible or necessary within the realm of practical relationship.

Should such an attack occur – one hesitates to say where such an armed attack could come from – the initial reliance must be on the people attacked to resist it and then upon the commitments of the entire civilized world under the Charter of the United Nations which so far has not proved a weak reed to lean on by any people who are determined to protect their independence against outside aggression. But it is a mistake, I think, in considering Pacific and Far Eastern problems to become obsessed with military considerations. Important as they are, there are other problems that press, and these other problems are not capable of solution through military means. . . .

So after this survey, what we conclude, I believe, is that there is a new day which has dawned in Asia. It is a day in which the Asian peoples are on their own, and know it, and intend to continue on their own. It is a day in which the old relationships between east and west are gone, relationships which at their worst were exploitations, and which at their best were paternalism. That relationship is over, and the relationship of east and west must now be in the Far East one of mutual respect and mutual helpfulness. We are their friends. Others are their friends. We and those others are willing to help, but we can help only where we

---

[3] Islands southwest of Japan.

are wanted and only where the conditions of help are really sensible and possible. So what we can see is that this new day in Asia, this new day which is dawning, may go on to a glorious noon or it may darken and it may drizzle out. But that decision lies within the countries of Asia and within the power of the Asian people. It is not a decision which a friend or even an enemy from the outside can decide for them.

Document 5

Address to the League of Women Voters, Wheeling, West Virginia

Joseph McCarthy

February 9, 1950

Senator Joseph McCarthy (R-Wisc.) was not a well-known figure when he spoke on February 9, 1950 at an event in Wheeling, West Virginia, sponsored by the League of Women Voters. A first-term Republican senator from Wisconsin, McCarthy addressed issues of espionage, domestic communism, and subversion within the U.S. government. Although McCarthy was unaware of the Venona decoding project (see the introduction to Document 10), recent events had provided alternative evidence of Soviet espionage. On January 21, 1950, for example, a federal grand jury indicted Alger Hiss, a former State Department official, of perjury charges related to his spy work for the Soviet Union during the 1930s. Hiss, who had many defenders, vigorously denied the charge that he had been a spy. The fact that he was found guilty of lying, not espionage, left many questions unanswered. Had Hiss really aided the Soviet Union? How many spies remained unidentified? Were they still active?

McCarthy seized on these questions to make the sensational charge that 205 State Department employees were members of the Communist Party of the United States of America and that Secretary of State Dean Acheson (Document 4) was protecting them. No list of such persons existed. In subsequent speeches, McCarthy cited different numbers – eighty-one, then fifty-seven – without providing much corroboration.

Problems with McCarthy's evidence did not diminish the massive attention McCarthy and his speech received. (Nor did the existence of a federal employee loyalty program that Truman had implemented in 1947.) The Hiss case, the communist victory in China, and the Soviet development of atomic weapons fed the impression that the United States was losing the Cold War. According to McCarthy, subversives within the U.S. government were responsible for this sudden reversal of fortune.

For the next several years, McCarthy was a celebrity, leading numerous Senate investigations of government agencies in search of subversion. Most of the people whom McCarthy accused of being communists were innocent of espionage. (Of the 159 individuals McCarthy named on his various lists, only nine were later identified by the Venona decoding project as having helped the Soviet Union; as noted, McCarthy did not have access to this information.) His anti-communist campaign was the centerpiece of the Cold War's Red Scare. His methods – the skillful use of the media, insinuations, and smears – earned the negative label of "McCarthyism" and contributed to the polarization of domestic politics. However, the undeniable evidence that numerous Americans had, in fact, spied for the Soviet Union kept the issue of subversion alive. McCarthy's recklessness and over-reach, especially his 1954 investigation of communism within the U.S. Army, led to his downfall (Document 7). He died in 1957 at age 48 from complications caused by heavy drinking.

Source: McCarthy spoke from a prepared text, but he apparently deviated from it at points and a tape recording was erased. This version comes from a copy provided to a Senate committee that investigated McCarthy's charges later that year. See Arthur M. Schlesinger, Jr., and Roger Bruns, eds., Congress Investigates: A Documented History, 1792-1974, Vol. 5 *(New York: Chelsea House Publishers, 1975), 3757–63.*

Ladies and gentlemen, tonight as we celebrate the one hundred forty-first birthday of one of the greatest men [*Abraham Lincoln*] in American history, I would like to be able to talk about what a glorious day today is in the history of the world. As we celebrate the birth of this man who with his whole heart and soul hated war, I would like to be able to speak of peace in our time – of war being outlawed – and of world-wide disarmament. These would be truly appropriate things to be able to mention as we celebrate the birthday of Abraham Lincoln.

Five years after a world war has been won, men's hearts should anticipate a long peace – and men's minds should be free from the heavy weight that comes with war. But this is not such a period – for this is not a period of peace. This is a time of the cold war. This is a time when all the world is split into two vast, increasingly hostile, armed camps – a time of a great armament race.

Today we can almost physically hear the mutterings and rumblings of an invigorated god of war. You can see it, feel it, and hear it all the way from the Indochina[1] hills, from the shores of Formosa [*Taiwan*], right over into the very heart of Europe itself.

The one encouraging thing is that the mad moment has not yet arrived for the firing of the gun or the exploding of the bomb which will set civilization about the final task of destroying itself. There is still a hope for peace if we finally decide that no longer can we safely blind our eyes and close our ears to those facts which are shaping up more and more clearly – and that is that we are now

---

[1] Indochina refers to the southeast Asian peninsula that includes the present-day nations of Burma (Myanmar), Malaya, Thailand, Vietnam, Laos, and Cambodia.

engaged in a show-down fight – not the usual war between nations for land areas or other material gains, but a war between two diametrically opposed ideologies.

The great difference between our western Christian world and the atheistic Communist world is not political, gentlemen, it is moral. For instance, the Marxian idea of confiscating the land and factories and running the entire economy as a single enterprise is momentous. Likewise, Lenin's[2] invention of the one-party police state as a way to make Marx's idea work is hardly less momentous.

Stalin's[3] resolute putting across of these two ideas, of course, did much to divide the world. With only these differences, however, the east and the west could most certainly still live in peace.

The real, basic difference, however, lies in the religion of immoralism – invented by Marx, preached feverishly by Lenin, and carried to unimaginable extremes by Stalin. This religion of immoralism, if the Red half of the world triumphs – and well it may, gentlemen – this religion of immoralism will more deeply wound and damage mankind than any conceivable economic or political system. . . .

Today we are engaged in a final, all-out battle between communistic atheism and Christianity. The modern champions of communism have selected this as the time, and ladies and gentlemen, the chips are down – they are truly down. . . .

Ladies and gentlemen, can there be anyone tonight who is so blind as to say that the war is not on? Can there be anyone who fails to realize that the Communist world has said the time is now – that this is the time for the show-down between the democratic Christian world and the communistic atheistic world?

Unless we face this fact, we shall pay the price that must be paid by those who wait too long.

Six years ago . . . there was within the Soviet orbit, 180,000,000 people. Lined up on the anti-totalitarian side there were in the world at that time, roughly 1,625,000,000 people. Today, only six years later, there are 80,000,000,000 people under the absolute domination of Soviet Russia – an increase of over 400 percent. On our side, the figure has shrunk to around

---

[2] Vladimir Lenin, a leader of the Russian Revolution and an important communist theorist.

[3] Josef Stalin, leader of the Soviet Union.

500,000. In other words, in less than six years, the odds have changed from 9 to 1 in our favor to 8 to 1 against us.[4]

This indicates the swiftness of the tempo of Communist victories and American defeats in the cold war. As one of our outstanding historical figures once said, "When a great democracy is destroyed, it will not be from enemies from without, but rather because of enemies from within" ... [5]

The reason why we find ourselves in a position of impotency is not because our only powerful potential enemy has sent men to invade our shores – but rather because of the traitorous actions of those who have been treated so well by this Nation. It has not been the less fortunate, or members of minority groups who have been traitorous to this Nation – but rather those who have had all the benefits that the wealthiest Nation on earth has had to offer – the finest homes, the finest college education and the finest jobs in government we can give.

This is glaringly true in the State Department. There the bright young men who are born with silver spoons in their mouths are the ones who have been most traitorous....

... I have here in my hand a list of 205 – a list of names that were made known to the Secretary of State as being members of the Communist Party and who nevertheless are still working and shaping policy in the State Department. . . .

As you know, very recently the Secretary of State [Dean Acheson] proclaimed his loyalty to a man guilty[6] of what has always been considered as the most abominable of all crimes – being a traitor to the people who gave him a position of great trust – high treason....

He has lighted the spark which is resulting in a moral uprising and will end only when the whole sorry mess of twisted, warped thinkers are swept from the national scene so that we may have a new birth of honesty and decency in government.

---

[4] McCarthy's population statistics are grossly wrong. He claims, for example, that 80 billion people live under the "absolute domination" of the Soviet Union; in 1950, the total world population was approximately 2.5 billion.

[5] McCarthy did not identify the speaker of the quote. He may be referring to a speech Abraham Lincoln delivered in 1838, but what Lincoln actually said was, "If destruction be our lot, we must ourselves be its author and finisher." See "The Perpetuation of Our Political Institutions: Address Before the Young Men's Lyceum of Springfield, Illinois," January 27, 1838.

[6] Alger Hiss (see introductory note).

Document 6

United States Objectives and Programs for National Security (NSC 68)

National Security Council

April 7, 1950

The bureaucratic title of this document hides its extraordinary influence. Produced under the authority of the National Security Council, an advisory body created as part of the National Security Act of 1947, this policy paper helped to militarize containment and to drastically increase defense spending. The scope of the paper was ambitious and wide-ranging; some parts resembled a doctoral thesis more than a policy document. Its primary author was Paul Nitze, who replaced George Kennan as the head of the State Department's Policy Planning Staff (Document 1). Secretary of State Dean Acheson gave this assignment to Nitze in part because he favorably anticipated that Nitze would recommend a bold new approach to fighting the Cold War. Indeed, Nitze recommended that the United States swiftly marshal all of its resources to build up the political, economic, and military strength of itself and its allies in order to counter Soviet expansion. From the perspective of NSC 68, a more aggressive version of containment was necessary to overcome the perceived threat.

In June 1950, the North Korean attack on South Korea (Documents 8–9) seemed to show the truth of Nitze's analysis of the Soviet Union as aggressive and seeking world domination. Although the Soviet Union had not ordered the invasion, Truman and his top policymakers believed the Soviets were responsible and that they might order invasions elsewhere, especially in Western Europe. The Korean War delayed action on NSC 68 but also clinched its acceptance. When the president signed NSC 68 in September 1950, he indicated that it should be the foundation of U.S. national security for the next several years. Accordingly, defense spending rose. In the spring of 1950, the amount requested for military services was less than $13 billion; in 1951, that figure exceeded $60 billion.

Source: NSC 68, United States Objectives and Programs for National Security [Document 85], The Foreign Relations of the United States, 1950, National Security Affairs, Vol. I, Foreign Economic Policy (Washington, D.C.: U.S. Department of State, Office of the Historian, 1977). Available at https://goo.gl/VhnMN8.

The following report is submitted in response to the President's directive of January 31 which reads:

"That the President direct the Secretary of State and the Secretary of Defense to undertake a reexamination of our objectives in peace and war and of the effect of these objectives on our strategic plans, in the light of the probable fission bomb capability and possible thermonuclear bomb capability of the Soviet Union."[1] ...

ANALYSIS

I. Background of the Present Crisis
Within the past thirty-five years the world has experienced two global wars of tremendous violence. It has witnessed two revolutions – the Russian and the Chinese – of extreme scope and intensity. It has also seen the collapse of five empires – the Ottoman, the Austro-Hungarian, German, Italian, and Japanese – and the drastic decline of two major imperial systems, the British and the French. During the span of one generation, the international distribution of power has been fundamentally altered....

... [T]he Soviet Union ... is animated by a new fanatic faith [communism], antithetical to our own, and seeks to impose its absolute authority over the rest of the world. Conflict has, therefore, become endemic and is waged, on the part of the Soviet Union, by violent or non-violent methods in accordance with the dictates of expediency. With the development of increasingly terrifying weapons of mass destruction, every individual faces the ever-present possibility of annihilation should the conflict enter the phase of total war....

The issues that face us are momentous, involving the fulfillment or destruction not only of this Republic but of civilization itself. They are issues which will not await our deliberations. With conscience and resolution this Government and the people it represents must now take new and fateful decisions.

II. Fundamental Purpose of the United States
The fundamental purpose of the United States is laid down in the Preamble to the Constitution: " ... to form a more perfect Union, establish Justice, insure domestic Tranquility, provide for the common defence, promote the general Welfare, and secure the Blessings of Liberty to ourselves and our Posterity." In

---

[1] A fission bomb, also known as an atomic bomb, was the type used against Japan in 1945. Thermonuclear or hydrogen bombs are much more powerful than atomic weapons. The United States first tested a hydrogen bomb in 1952; the Soviet Union, in 1953.

essence, the fundamental purpose is to assure the integrity and vitality of our free society, which is founded upon the dignity and worth of the individual.

Three realities emerge as a consequence of this purpose: Our determination to maintain the essential elements of individual freedom, as set forth in the Constitution and Bill of Rights; our determination to create conditions under which our free and democratic system can live and prosper; and our determination to fight if necessary to defend our way of life, for which as in the Declaration of Independence, "with a firm reliance on the protection of Divine Providence, we mutually pledge to each other our lives, our Fortunes, and our sacred Honor."

III. Fundamental Design of the Kremlin

The fundamental design of those who control the Soviet Union and the international communist movement is to retain and solidify their absolute power, first in the Soviet Union and second in the areas now under their control. In the minds of the Soviet leaders, however, achievement of this design requires the dynamic extension of their authority and the ultimate elimination of any effective opposition to their authority.

The design, therefore, calls for the complete subversion or forcible destruction of the machinery of government and structure of society in the countries of the non-Soviet world and their replacement by an apparatus and structure subservient to and controlled from the Kremlin. To that end Soviet efforts are now directed toward the domination of the Eurasian land mass. The United States, as the principal center of power in the non-Soviet world and the bulwark of opposition to Soviet expansion, is the principal enemy whose integrity and vitality must be subverted or destroyed by one means or another if the Kremlin is to achieve its fundamental design.

IV. The Underlying Conflict in the Realm of Ideas and Values between the U.S. Purpose and the Kremlin Design

A. *Nature of Conflict*

The Kremlin regards the United States as the only major threat to the achievement of its fundamental design. There is a basic conflict between the idea of freedom under a government of laws, and the idea of slavery under the grim oligarchy of the Kremlin, which has come to a crisis with the polarization of power described in Section I, and the exclusive possession of atomic weapons by the two protagonists. . . .

. . . Unwillingly our free society finds itself mortally challenged by the Soviet system. No other value system is so wholly irreconcilable with ours, so implacable in its purpose to destroy ours, so capable of turning to its own uses the most dangerous and divisive trends in our own society, no other so skillfully and powerfully evokes the elements of irrationality in human nature everywhere, and no other has the support of a great and growing center of military power.

B. *Objectives*

The objectives of a free society are determined by its fundamental values and by the necessity for maintaining the material environment in which they flourish. Logically and in fact, therefore, the Kremlin's challenge to the United States is directed not only to our values but to our physical capacity to protect their environment. It is a challenge which encompasses both peace and war and our objectives in peace and war must take account of it. . . .

In a shrinking world, which now faces the threat of atomic warfare, it is not an adequate objective merely to seek to check the Kremlin design, for the absence of order among nations is becoming less and less tolerable. This fact imposes on us, in our own interests, the responsibility of world leadership. It demands that we make the attempt, and accept the risks inherent in it, to bring about order and justice by means consistent with the principles of freedom and democracy. . . .

C. *Means*

The free society is limited in its choice of means to achieve its ends.

. . . Resort to war is not only a last resort for a free society, but it is also an act which cannot definitively end the fundamental conflict in the realm of ideas. The idea of slavery can only be overcome by the timely and persistent demonstration of the superiority of the idea of freedom. Military victory alone would only partially and perhaps only temporarily affect the fundamental conflict, for although the ability of the Kremlin to threaten our security might be for a time destroyed, the resurgence of totalitarian forces and the re-establishment of the Soviet system or its equivalent would not be long delayed unless great progress were made in the fundamental conflict.

Practical and ideological considerations therefore both impel us to the conclusion that we have no choice but to demonstrate the superiority of the idea of freedom by its constructive application, and to attempt to change the world situation by means short of war in such a way as to frustrate the Kremlin design and hasten the decay of the Soviet system.

For us the role of military power is to serve the national purpose by deterring an attack upon us while we seek by other means to create an environment in which our free society can flourish, and by fighting, if necessary, to defend the integrity and vitality of our free society and to defeat any aggressor. The Kremlin uses Soviet military power to back up and serve the Kremlin design. It does not hesitate to use military force aggressively if that course is expedient in the achievement of its design. The differences between our fundamental purpose and the Kremlin design, therefore, are reflected in our respective attitudes toward and use of military force.

Our free society, confronted by a threat to its basic values, naturally will take such action, including the use of military force, as may be required to protect those values....

... Our aim in applying force must be to compel the acceptance of terms consistent with our objectives, and our capabilities for the application of force should, therefore, within the limits of what we can sustain over the long pull, be congruent to the range of tasks which we may encounter.

V. Soviet Intentions and Capabilities

A. *Political and Psychological*

The Kremlin's design for world domination begins at home. The first concern of a despotic oligarchy is that the local base of its power and authority be secure....

Being a totalitarian dictatorship, the Kremlin's objective in these policies is the total subjective submission of the peoples now under its control....

The Kremlin's policy toward areas not under its control is the elimination of resistance to its will and the extension of its influence and control. It is driven to follow this policy because it cannot ... tolerate the existence of free societies; to the Kremlin the most mild and inoffensive free society is an affront, a challenge and a subversive influence....

With particular reference to the United States, the Kremlin's strategic and tactical policy is affected by its estimate that we are not only the greatest immediate obstacle which stands between it and world domination, we are also the only power which could release forces in the free and Soviet worlds which could destroy it. The Kremlin's policy toward us is consequently animated by a peculiarly virulent blend of hatred and fear....

B. *Economic*

The Kremlin has no economic intentions unrelated to its overall policies. Economics in the Soviet world is not an end in itself. The Kremlin's policy, in so far as it has to do with economics, is to utilize economic processes to contribute to the overall strength, particularly the war-making capacity of the Soviet system. The material welfare of the totalitariat[2] is severely subordinated to the interest of the system....

---

[2] A play on the Marxist term "proletariat" (the lowest class of workers within a capitalist economy), "totalitariat" means those living within the totalitarian system of the Soviet Union.

C. Military

The Soviet Union is developing the military capacity to support its design for world domination. The Soviet Union actually possesses armed forces far in excess of those necessary to defend its national territory. These armed forces are probably not yet considered by the Soviet Union to be sufficient to initiate a war which would involve the United States. This excessive strength, coupled now with an atomic capability, provides the Soviet Union with great coercive power for use in time of peace in furtherance of its objectives and serves as a deterrent to the victims of its aggression from taking any action in opposition to its tactics which would risk war.

Should a major war occur in 1950 the Soviet Union and its satellites are considered by the Joint Chiefs of Staff to be in a sufficiently advanced state of preparation immediately to undertake and carry out the following campaigns.

a. To overrun Western Europe, with the possible exception of the Iberian and Scandinavian Peninsulas; to drive toward the oil-bearing areas of the Near and Middle East; and to consolidate Communist gains in the Far East;

b. To launch air attacks against the British Isles and air and sea attacks against the lines of communications of the Western Powers in the Atlantic and the Pacific;

c. To attack selected targets with atomic weapons, now including the likelihood of such attacks against targets in Alaska, Canada, and the United States. Alternatively, this capability, coupled with other actions open to the Soviet Union, might deny the United Kingdom as an effective base of operations for allied forces. It also should be possible for the Soviet Union to prevent any allied "Normandy" type amphibious operations intended to force a reentry into the continent of Europe. . . .

VI. U.S. Intentions and Capabilities – Actual and Potential

A. Political and Psychological

. . . In "containment" it is desirable to exert pressure in a fashion which will avoid so far as possible directly challenging Soviet prestige, to keep open the possibility for the U.S.S.R. to retreat before pressure with a minimum loss of face and to secure political advantage from the failure of the Kremlin to yield or take advantage of the opening we leave it.

We have failed to implement adequately these two fundamental aspects of "containment." In the face of obviously mounting Soviet military strength ours has declined relatively. Partly as a byproduct of this, but also for other reasons, we now find ourselves at a diplomatic impasse with the Soviet Union, with the Kremlin growing bolder, with both of us holding on grimly to what we have and with ourselves facing difficult decisions. . . .

Document 7

Declaration of Conscience
Margaret Chase Smith
June 1, 1950

When Senator Joseph McCarthy faltered in supporting his 1950 charge that the State Department knowingly employed more than 200 communists (Document 5), numerous Republican members of Congress backed him up. The problem of Soviet espionage was a real one, and the attention McCarthy received enhanced conservatives' criticism that the Truman administration had not adequately dealt with the issue. However, not all Republicans approved of McCarthy's methods, especially his harsh attacks on critics. In June 1950, Senator Margaret Chase Smith (R-Maine) spoke out against McCarthy's "selfish political exploitation," though she was careful not to identify him by name.

Smith persuaded six fellow Republicans to sign this Declaration of Conscience, which ended with a call for bipartisan cooperation to protect national security. The declaration had very little immediate effect, but it opened a pathway for Republicans to later break with McCarthy because of his methods. After the Wisconsin senator charged Army officers with harboring communists, Republican President Dwight D. Eisenhower began working behind the scenes with Congressional Republicans to isolate him and diminish his influence. These efforts culminated in a Senate censure in December 1954 for actions "contrary to senatorial traditions." His power gone and his reputation irreparably harmed, McCarthy died less than three years later.

Source: Congressional Record, *81st Congress, 2d sess., pp. 7894-95. Available at https://goo.gl/CR8cPU.*

Mr. President, I would like to speak briefly and simply about a serious national condition. It is a national feeling of fear and frustration that could result in national suicide and the end of everything that we Americans hold dear. It is a condition that comes from the lack of effective leadership either in the legislative branch or the executive branch of our government. . . .

. . . I speak as a Republican. I speak as a woman. I speak as a United States senator. I speak as an American. . . .

. . . I think that it is high time for the United States Senate and its members to do some real soul searching and to weigh our consciences as to the manner in which we are performing our duty to the people of America and the manner in which we are using or abusing our individual powers and privileges.

I think that it is high time that we remembered that we have sworn to uphold and defend the Constitution. I think that it is high time that we remembered that the Constitution, as amended, speaks not only of the freedom of speech, but also of trial by jury instead of trial by accusation.

Whether it be a criminal prosecution in court or a character prosecution in the Senate, there is little practical distinction when the life of a person has been ruined.

"The Basic Principles of Americanism"

Those of us who shout the loudest about Americanism in making character assassinations are all too frequently those who, by our own words and acts, ignore some of the basic principles of Americanism –

The right to criticize.

The right to hold unpopular beliefs.

The right to protest.

The right of independent thought.

The exercise of these rights should not cost one single American citizen his reputation or his right to a livelihood nor should he be in danger of losing his reputation or livelihood merely because he happens to know someone who holds unpopular beliefs. Who of us does not? Otherwise none of us could call our souls our own. Otherwise thought control would have set in.

The American people are sick and tired of being afraid to speak their minds lest they be politically smeared as "Communists" or "Fascists"[1] by their opponents. Freedom of speech is not what it used to be in America. It has been so abused by some that it is not exercised by others.

The American people are sick and tired of seeing innocent people smeared and guilty people whitewashed. But there have been enough proved cases ... to cause nationwide distrust and strong suspicion that there may be something to the unproved, sensational accusations.

A Challenge to the Republican Party

As a Republican, I say to my colleagues on this side of the aisle that the Republican party faces a challenge today that is not unlike the challenge that it

---

[1] Fascism is a political ideology based on intense nationalism, glorification of war and violence, and suppression of freedom. Germany under Nazi rule was, for example, a fascist state. Fascism is strongly anti-communist – Nazi Germany tried to destroy the Soviet Union during World War II – even though communism and fascism often both use the same methods to take away citizens' freedoms.

faced back in Lincoln's day. The Republican Party so successfully met that challenge that it emerged from the Civil War as the champion of a united nation – in addition to being a party that unrelentingly fought loose spending and loose programs . . . .

The Democratic administration[2] has greatly lost the confidence of the American people by its complacency to the threat of communism here at home and the leak of vital secrets to Russia through key officials of the Democratic administration. There are enough proved cases to make this point without diluting our criticism with unproved charges.

Surely these are sufficient reasons to make it clear to the American people that it is time for a change and that a Republican victory is necessary to the security of this country . . . . Yet to displace it with a Republican regime embracing a philosophy that lacks political integrity or intellectual honesty would prove equally disastrous to this Nation. The nation sorely needs a Republican victory. But I do not want to see the Republican party ride to political victory . . . [using] fear, ignorance, bigotry, and smear . . . I do not want to see the Republican party win that way. While it might be a fleeting victory for the Republican party, it would be a more lasting defeat for the American people. Surely it would ultimately be suicide for the Republican party and the two-party system that has protected our American liberties from the dictatorship of a one-party system.

As members of the minority party, we do not have the primary authority to formulate the policy of our government. But we do have the responsibility of rendering constructive criticism, of clarifying issues, of allaying fears by acting as responsible citizens.

As a woman, I wonder how the mothers, wives, sisters, and daughters feel about the way in which members of their families have been politically mangled in Senate debate – and I use the word "debate" advisedly . . .

I do not like the way the Senate has been made a rendezvous for vilification, for selfish political gain at the sacrifice of individual reputations and national unity. I am not proud of the way we smear outsiders from the floor of the Senate and hide behind the cloak of congressional immunity and still place ourselves beyond criticism on the floor of the Senate.

As an American, I am shocked at the way Republicans and Democrats alike are playing directly into the Communist design of "confuse, divide, and conquer." As an American, I don't want a Democratic administration "whitewash" or "cover-up" any more than I want a Republican smear or witch hunt.

---

[2] Truman administration.

As an American, I condemn a Republican Fascist just as much as I condemn a Democrat Communist. I condemn a Democrat Fascist just as much as I condemn a Republican Communist. They are equally dangerous to you and me and to our country. As an American, I want to see our nation recapture the strength and unity it once had when we fought the enemy instead of ourselves.

It is with these thoughts I have drafted what I call a Declaration of Conscience. I am gratified that the senator from New Hampshire, the senator from Vermont, the senator from Oregon, the senator from New York, the senator from Minnesota and the senator from New Jersey have concurred in that declaration and have authorized me to announce their concurrence.

The declaration reads as follows:

Statement of Seven Republican Senators[3]

1. We are Republicans. But we are Americans first. It is as Americans that we express our concern with the growing confusion that threatens the security and stability of our country. Democrats and Republicans alike have contributed to that confusion.

2. The Democratic administration has initially created the confusion by its lack of effective leadership, by its contradictory grave warnings and optimistic assurances, by its complacency to the threat of communism here at home, by its oversensitiveness to rightful criticism, by its petty bitterness against its critics.

3. Certain elements of the Republican party have materially added to this confusion in the hopes of riding the Republican party to victory through the selfish political exploitation of fear, bigotry, ignorance, and intolerance. There are enough mistakes of the Democrats for Republicans to criticize constructively without resorting to political smears.

4. To this extent, Democrats and Republicans alike have unwittingly, but undeniably, played directly into the Communist design of "confuse, divide, and conquer."

5. It is high time that we stopped thinking politically as Republicans and Democrats about elections and started thinking patriotically as Americans about national security based on individual freedom. It is high time that we all stopped being tools and victims of totalitarian techniques – techniques that, if continued here unchecked, will surely end what we have come to cherish as the American way of life.

---

[3] The seven Republican senators were Charles Tobey (R-N.H.), George Aiken (R-Vt.), Wayne Morse (R-Ore.), Irving Ives (R-N.Y.), Edward Thye (R-Minn.), and Robert Hendrickson (R-N.J.).

Documents 8 and 9

The Korean War
June 25, 1950 – July 27, 1953

The Korean War was the first major armed conflict of the Cold War. It tested the commitment of the United States to containment and raised a significant question about the end goal of the U.S. Cold War policy: should it seek only to stop the spread of communism or should it also try to roll back communism? Unexpected developments in the war led to a clash between President Harry Truman and his top general in Korea, Douglas MacArthur, as these documents show.

The war's origins lay in the troubled division of Korea into South Korea and North Korea following Japan's defeat in World War II, which brought to an end the Japanese occupation of Korea (1910 – 1945). North Korea was communist; the South anti-communist.

On June 25, 1950, North Korean forces carried out a massive invasion of the South. Soviet leader Josef Stalin had approved of – but had not ordered – the action, but Soviet military aid to North Korea seemed to confirm the prediction of NSC 68 that the communists sought world domination (Document 6). President Truman, Secretary of State Dean Acheson, and top-level national security and military officials agreed that the United States and its allies must act immediately to protect South Korea. Although Acheson had suggested in January that the United States would not deploy its military forces outside of the so-called defensive perimeter in Asia (Document 4), he also stated that an attacked nation could rely on the United Nations. American military action was therefore enabled by U.N. Security Council decisions. U.N. forces in Korea included those from the United States and 16 other nations.

A risky amphibious landing at Inchon (September 1950), conceived and commanded by General Douglas MacArthur, turned the tide of battle in favor of U.N. forces, which advanced toward the line of division between the two Koreas, recovering ground lost to the North and then, with the urging of MacArthur, into North Korea itself, eventually approaching the border with China. In response to the U.N. advance, China sent its forces into North Korea (October 1950), causing the U.N. forces to retreat and leading eventually to a stalemate along the original line dividing North and South Korea.

Chinese intervention drastically raised the stakes of the war. If Truman ordered U.N. forces to retreat to South Korean territory, he risked criticism that the decision to invade North Korea was a mistake. But efforts to force a Chinese withdrawal were certain to prolong the war and result in increased U.S. casualties. Aggressive statements by MacArthur calling for a direct attack on China further complicated Truman's position. Truman decided to relieve MacArthur of his command for insubordination. (The general had defied orders that he clear his public statements with the White House before their release.) Truman announced his decision on April 11, 1951, the day he also delivered this speech (Document 8).

MacArthur did not go quietly. Congressional leaders invited him to address both houses, and the general used the occasion to defend his ideas for winning the Korean War (Document 9). MacArthur famously declared, "In war there is no substitute for victory." Hailed as a hero, he embarked on a national tour, basking in the cheers of adoring crowds in numerous cities. He briefly flirted with running for president as a Republican but soon faded from public view. Truman's popularity fell, but in hindsight his decision to protect the chain of command was a wise one. What hurt Truman more was the grinding stalemate of the Korean War. With his approval ratings at an all-time low, he decided not to seek re-election in 1952. The task of ending the war fell to his successor, Republican Dwight D. Eisenhower, who brokered a cease-fire in July 1953 that restored the prewar situation: Korea remained divided; a communist regime still held power in the North.

Source: Report to the American People on Korea, University of Virginia, Miller Center. April 11, 1951. Available at https://goo.gl/5eM2yQ.

Source: MacArthur Speech, Transcript of General Douglas MacArthur's Address to Congress, April 19, 1951. Available at https://goo.gl/9m6hFR.

Document 8

Report to the American People on Korea
President Harry S. Truman
April 11, 1951

I want to talk to you plainly tonight about what we are doing in Korea and about our policy in the Far East.

In the simplest terms, what we are doing in Korea is this: We are trying to prevent a third world war.

I think most people in this country recognized that fact last June. And they warmly supported the decision of the Government to help the Republic of Korea against the Communist aggressors. . . .

The Communists in the Kremlin are engaged in a monstrous conspiracy to stamp out freedom all over the world. If they were to succeed, the United States would be numbered among their principal victims. It must be clear to everyone that the United States cannot – and will not – sit idly by and await foreign conquest. The only question is: What is the best time to meet the threat and how is the best way to meet it?

The best time to meet the threat is in the beginning. It is easier to put out a fire in the beginning when it is small than after it has become a roaring blaze. And the best way to meet the threat of aggression is for the peace-loving nations to act together. If they don't act together, they are likely to be picked off, one by one.

If they had followed the right policies in the 1930's – if the free countries had acted together to crush the aggression of the dictators, and if they had acted in the beginning when the aggression was small – there probably would have been no World War II.

If history has taught us anything, it is that aggression anywhere in the world is a threat to the peace everywhere in the world. When that aggression is supported by the cruel and selfish rulers of a powerful nation who are bent on conquest, it becomes a clear and present danger to the security and independence of every free nation.

This is a lesson that most people in this country have learned thoroughly. This is the basic reason why we joined in creating the United Nations. And, since the end of World War II, we have been putting that lesson into practice – we have been working with other free nations to check the aggressive designs of the Soviet Union before they can result in a third world war.

That is what we did in Greece, when that nation was threatened by the aggression of international communism.[1]

The attack against Greece could have led to general war. But this country came to the aid of Greece. The United Nations supported Greek resistance. With our help, the determination and efforts of the Greek people defeated the attack on the spot. . . .

The aggression against Korea is the boldest and most dangerous move the Communists have yet made.

The attack on Korea was part of a greater plan for conquering all of Asia.

. . .

This plan of conquest is in flat contradiction to what we believe. We believe that Korea belongs to the Koreans, we believe that India belongs to the Indians, we believe that all the nations of Asia should be free to work out their affairs in their own way. This is the basis of peace in the Far East, and it is the basis of peace everywhere else. . . .

The question we have had to face is whether the Communist plan of conquest can be stopped without a general war. Our Government and other countries associated with us in the United Nations believe that the best chance of stopping it without a general war is to meet the attack in Korea and defeat it there.

That is what we have been doing. It is a difficult and bitter task.

But so far it has been successful.

So far, we have prevented world war III.

So far, by fighting a limited war in Korea, we have prevented aggression from succeeding, and bringing on a general war. And the ability of the whole free world to resist Communist aggression has been greatly improved.

We have taught the enemy a lesson. He has found that aggression is not cheap or easy. Moreover, men all over the world who want to remain free have been given new courage and new hope. They know now that the champions of freedom can stand up and fight, and that they will stand up and fight. . . .

The Communist side must now choose its course of action. The Communist rulers may press the attack against us. They may take further action which will spread the conflict. They have that choice, and with it the awful responsibility for what may follow. The Communists also have the choice of a peaceful settlement which could lead to a general relaxation of the tensions in the Far East. The decision is theirs, because the forces of the United Nations will strive to limit the conflict if possible. . . .

---

[1] See Document 2.

But you may ask why can't we take other steps to punish the aggressor. Why don't we bomb Manchuria[2] and China itself? Why don't we assist the Chinese Nationalist troops to land on the mainland of China?[3]

If we were to do these things we would be running a very grave risk of starting a general war. If that were to happen, we would have brought about the exact situation we are trying to prevent.

If we were to do these things, we would become entangled in a vast conflict on the continent of Asia and our task would become immeasurably more difficult all over the world. . . .

Our aim is to avoid the spread of the conflict.

The course we have been following is the one best calculated to avoid an all-out war. It is the course consistent with our obligation to do all we can to maintain international peace and security. Our experience in Greece . . . shows that it is the most effective course of action we can follow.

First of all, it is clear that our efforts in Korea can blunt the will of the Chinese Communists to continue the struggle. The United Nations forces have put up a tremendous fight in Korea and have inflicted very heavy casualties on the enemy. Our forces are stronger now than they have been before. These are plain facts which may discourage the Chinese Communists from continuing their attack.

Second, the free world as a whole is growing in military strength every day. In the United States, in Western Europe, and throughout the world, free men are alert to the Soviet threat and are building their defenses. This may discourage the Communist rulers from continuing the war in Korea – and from undertaking new acts of aggression elsewhere.

If the Communist authorities realize that they cannot defeat us in Korea, if they realize it would be foolhardy to widen the hostilities beyond Korea, then they may recognize the folly of continuing their aggression. A peaceful settlement may then be possible. The door is always open.

Then we may achieve a settlement in Korea which will not compromise the principles and purposes of the United Nations.

I have thought long and hard about this question of extending the war in Asia. I have discussed it many times with the ablest military advisers in the country. I believe with all my heart that the course we are following is the best course.

I believe that we must try to limit the war to Korea for these vital reasons: to make sure that the precious lives of our fighting men are not wasted; to see

---

[2] Northern China.

[3] After losing China's civil war to the communists, the Chinese nationalists – whom the United States had supported – retreated to the island of Taiwan, then called Formosa.

that the security of our country and the free world is not needlessly jeopardized; and to prevent a third world war.

A number of events have made it evident that General MacArthur did not agree with that policy. I have therefore considered it essential to relieve General MacArthur so that there would be no doubt or confusion as to the real purpose and aim of our policy.

It was with the deepest personal regret that I found myself compelled to take this action. General MacArthur is one of our greatest military commanders. But the cause of world peace is much more important than any individual.

The change in commands in the Far East means no change whatever in the policy of the United States. We will carry on the fight in Korea with vigor and determination in an effort to bring the war to a speedy and successful conclusion. . . .

Document 9

Address to Congress
Douglas D. MacArthur
April 19, 1951

Mr. President, Mr. Speaker and distinguished members of the Congress:

I stand on this rostrum with a sense of deep humility and great pride – humility in the wake of those great architects of our history who have stood here before me, pride in the reflection that this home of legislative debate represents human liberty in the purest form yet devised.

Here are centered the hopes and aspirations and faith of the entire human race.

I do not stand here as advocate for any partisan cause, for the issues are fundamental and reach quite beyond the realm of partisan considerations. They must be resolved on the highest plane of national interest if our course is to prove sound and our future protected. . . .

The issues are global, and so interlocked that to consider the problems of one sector oblivious to those of another is to court disaster for the whole. While Asia is commonly referred to as the gateway to Europe, it is no less true that Europe is the gateway to Asia, and the broad influence of the one cannot fail to have its impact upon the other. There are those who claim our strength is inadequate to protect on both fronts, that we cannot divide our effort. I can think of no greater expression of defeatism.

If a potential enemy can divide his strength on two fronts, it is for us to counter his efforts. The Communist threat is a global one.

Its successful advance in one sector threatens the destruction of every other sector. You cannot appease or otherwise surrender to communism in Asia without simultaneously undermining our efforts to halt its advance in Europe. . . .

While I was not consulted prior to the President's decision to intervene in support of the Republic of Korea, that decision, from a military standpoint, proved a sound one. As I said, it proved to be a sound one, as we hurled back the invader and decimated his forces. Our victory was complete, and our objectives within reach, when Red China intervened with numerically superior ground forces.

This created a new war and an entirely new situation, a situation not contemplated when our forces were committed against the North Korean invaders; a situation which called for new decisions in the diplomatic sphere to permit the realistic adjustment of military strategy. Such decisions have not been forthcoming.

While no man in his right mind would advocate sending our ground forces into continental China, and such was never given a thought, the new situation did urgently demand a drastic revision of strategic planning if our political aim was to defeat this new enemy as we had defeated the old.

Apart from the military need, as I saw it, to neutralize the sanctuary protection given the enemy north of the Yalu,[1] I felt that military necessity in the conduct of the war made necessary

(1) the intensification of our economic blockade against China,; (2) the imposition of a naval blockade against the China coast; (3) removal of restrictions on air reconnaissance of China's coastal area and of Manchuria; (4) removal of restrictions on the forces of the Republic of China on Formosa, with logistical support to contribute to their effective operations against the Chinese mainland.

For entertaining these views, all professionally designed to support our forces in Korea and to bring hostilities to an end with the least possible delay and at a saving of countless American and allied lives, I have been severely criticized in lay circles, principally abroad, despite my understanding that from a military standpoint the above views have been fully shared in the past by practically every military leader concerned with the Korean campaign, including our own Joint Chiefs of Staff.[2] . . .

We could hold in Korea by constant maneuver and in an approximate area where our supply line advantages were in balance with the supply line disadvantages of the enemy, but we could hope at best for only an indecisive campaign with its terrible and constant attrition upon our forces if the enemy utilized its full military potential.

I have constantly called for the new political decisions essential to a solution.

Efforts have been made to distort my position. It has been said in effect that I was a warmonger. Nothing could be further from the truth.

I know war as few other men now living know it, and nothing to me – and nothing to me is more revolting. I have long advocated its complete abolition,

---

[1] The Yalu River is the border between North Korea and China.
[2] The Joint Chiefs of Staff are the leaders of each of the military services. Through the chairman of the Joint Chiefs of Staff they advise the president.

as its very destructiveness on both friend and foe has rendered it useless as a means of settling international disputes. . . .

But once war is forced upon us, there is no other alternative than to apply every available means to bring it to a swift end. War's very object is victory, not prolonged indecision.

In war there is no substitute for victory.

There are some who for varying reasons would appease Red China.[3] They are blind to history's clear lesson, for history teaches with unmistakable emphasis that appeasement but begets new and bloodier war.[4] It points to no single instance where this end has justified that means, where appeasement had led to more than a sham peace. Like blackmail, it lays the basis for new and successively greater demands until, as in blackmail, violence becomes the only other alternative. Why, my soldiers asked me, surrender military advantages to an enemy in the field? I could not answer.

Some may say to avoid spread of the conflict into an all-out war with China. Others, to avoid Soviet intervention. Neither explanation seems valid, for China is already engaging with the maximum power it can commit, and the Soviet will not necessarily mesh its actions with our moves. Like a cobra, any new enemy will more likely strike whenever it feels that the relativity of military and other potentialities is in its favor on a worldwide basis.

The tragedy of Korea is further heightened by the fact that its military action was confined to its territorial limits. It condemns that nation, which it is our purpose to save, to suffer the devastating impact of full naval and air bombardment while the enemy's sanctuaries are fully protected from such attack and devastation.

Of the nations of the world, Korea alone, up to now, is the sole one which has risked its all against communism. The magnificence of the courage and fortitude of the Korean people defies description. They have chosen to risk death rather than slavery. Their last words to me were: "Don't scuttle the Pacific."[5]

I have just left your fighting sons in Korea. They have done their best there, and I can report to you without reservation that they are splendid in every way.

---

[3] That is, communist China.

[4] Here MacArthur appears to reference the 1938 Munich conference, where the leaders of France and Great Britain agreed to not block Nazi Germany's takeover of a portion of Czechoslovakia known as the Sudetenland. The agreement did not, of course, halt German expansionism. During the Cold War, the Munich conference became a metaphor for the danger and folly of trying to appease aggressive nations and leaders.

[5] That is, don't leave the war.

It was my constant effort to preserve them and end this savage conflict honorably and with the least loss of time and a minimum sacrifice of life. Its growing bloodshed has caused me the deepest anguish and anxiety. Those gallant men will remain often in my thoughts and in my prayers always.

I am closing my 52 years of military service. When I joined the Army, even before the turn of the century, it was the fulfillment of all my boyish hopes and dreams. The world has turned over many times since I took the oath at West Point, and the hopes and dreams have all long since vanished, but I still remember the refrain of one of the most popular barracks ballads of that day which proclaimed most proudly that old soldiers never die; they just fade away.

And like the old soldier of that ballad, I now close my military career and just fade away, an old soldier who tried to do his duty as God gave him the light to see that duty. Good Bye.

Document 10

Sentencing of Ethel and Julius Rosenberg
Irving Kaufman
April 5, 1951

During World War II, the U.S. Army Signal Security Agency undertook an ambitious project, called Venona, to decipher the code the Soviet Union used to protect its diplomatic cables (messages transmitted by radio). Detection of a slight recurrence of code enabled cryptanalysts to eventually crack through several layers of cipher. The top-secret project revealed the names and activities of numerous Soviet spies, including British physicist Klaus Fuchs. In 1950, British authorities arrested Fuchs, who admitted he had passed on valuable information about the atomic bomb to the Soviet Union during World War II. Fuchs's confession led to the identification of more spies, many of them Americans. One, Julius Rosenberg, was arrested by the FBI in June 1950. Rosenberg denied the charges of espionage. In January 1951, a federal grand jury indicted him and his wife, Ethel. Federal prosecutors announced their intent to seek the death penalty for the couple in hopes that Ethel, who did not directly take part in her husband's spy work, would offer evidence against Julius. Both Rosenbergs, however, held firm in their assertion of innocence.

The Rosenbergs' trial opened in March 1951 with Judge Irving Kaufman presiding. Ethel's brother David Greenglass, who had also been charged with espionage, offered substantial testimony regarding Julius's spy work and his sister's knowledge of it. Prosecutors did not use the Venona cables because the U.S. government did not want the Soviets to learn that the United States had decrypted their wartime transmissions. Instead, prosecutors relied on Greenglass's testimony, as well as that of another former spy, Elizabeth Bentley. Based on this evidence, the jury handed down a guilty verdict on March 29, 1951.

A few days later, Judge Kaufman sentenced the Rosenbergs to death. In this sentencing statement, Kaufman condemned the couple for betraying the United States.

Numerous appeals failed to overturn the verdict and sentence, which were controversial and prompted protests. The Rosenbergs had many defenders, who accused the federal government of framing the couple. President Dwight D. Eisenhower denied a last-minute appeal for a pardon, and on June 19, 1953, the Rosenbergs were executed. Neither ever admitted their guilt, but Soviet records have since confirmed that Julius spied for the Soviet Union and that his wife knew about this espionage.[1] Their deaths orphaned their two sons and added to the tensions in the United States brought by the fear of communism.

Source: A copy of the sentencing statement can be found in Jake Kobrick, "The Rosenberg Trial," Federal Judicial Center, Federal Judicial History Office, 2013, 50-1. Available at https://goo.gl/fG2QG1.

Citizens of this country who betray their fellow-countrymen can be under none of the delusions about the benignity of Soviet power that they might have been prior to World War II. The nature of Russian terrorism is now self-evident. Idealism as a rationale dissolves. . . .

I consider your crime worse than murder. Plain deliberate contemplated murder is dwarfed in magnitude by comparison with the crime you have committed. In committing the act of murder, the criminal kills only his victim. The immediate family is brought to grief and when justice is meted out the chapter is closed. But in your case, I believe your conduct in putting into the hands of the Russians the A-bomb [*atomic bomb*] years before our best scientists predicted Russia would perfect the bomb has already caused, in my opinion, the Communist aggression in Korea, with the resultant casualties exceeding 50,000 and who knows but that millions more of innocent people may pay the price of your treason. Indeed, by your betrayal you undoubtedly have altered the course of history to the disadvantage of our country. No one can say that we do not live in a constant state of tension. We have evidence of your treachery all around us every day – for the civilian defense activities throughout the nation are aimed at preparing us for an atom bomb attack. . . .

In the light of the circumstances, I feel that I must pass such sentence upon the principals in this diabolical conspiracy to destroy a God-fearing nation, which will determine with finality that this nation's security must remain inviolate; that traffic in military secrets, whether promoted by slavish devotion to a foreign ideology or by a desire for monetary gains must cease. . . .

---

[1] *For examples of this evidence, see National Security Agency, Venona Documents, 1944, especially the documents dated November 27, 1944 and December 16, 1944.* Available at https://goo.gl/QT8Grq and https://goo.gl/XRSdfc.

Document 11

The Negro in American Life (Guidance for the Voice of America)

U.S. State Department

February 5, 1952

During World War II, the United States government used international shortwave radio to broadcast to Europe and North Africa. Known as the Voice of America (VOA), the network promoted the war aims of the Allies, delivered news about the war, and offered features about life in the United States. The Cold War kept the VOA on the air, as the State Department recognized its potential to persuade listeners in other nations to support the United States and democracy. Public diplomacy – direct contact by a government with foreign populations – provided a way to explain and win supporters for containment and anti-communist policies. The Korean War (Documents 8–9) especially highlighted the usefulness of speaking to a global audience. VOA content became more hard-hitting as it countered Soviet claims that the United States and its allies were the aggressors in Korea.

The Soviet Union, which also engaged in public diplomacy, relentlessly criticized the United States for its segregation of and discrimination against African Americans. (In the early postwar period, the term Negro was still commonly used to refer to African Americans.) Although Soviet reporting was one-sided, no one could truthfully deny that African Americans did not as yet have equal opportunity and full civil rights in the United States. This document shows how the VOA tried to strike a balance in its coverage of this issue.

How much the VOA's calibrated coverage of African Americans affected foreign opinion is difficult to measure. The document is historically significant, though, because it reveals the growing importance of public diplomacy and mass media in the Cold War. Throughout the 1950s and 1960s, the United States and the Soviet Union both extensively used radio, print media, film, and television to reach and influence foreign populations. For another example of the importance of public diplomacy, see Document 18 (The Kitchen Debate).

Source: Record Group 59, Records of the Department of State, Records Relating to International Information Activities, 1938-1953, box 86, folder "Negroes," National Archives, College Park, MD.

The VOA coverage of the Negro in American life falls into three categories:
1. Features and News items dealing with the Negro in America
2. The Negro and Politics
3. The Negro and Art

<u>Features and News</u> – By and large, American Negroes receive steady mention in VOA's regular output of domestic news items. In fact, a check shows that at least once every three days Negro achievements and personalities are mentioned in our American Roundup circulated in all languages desks. Typical examples would be:

A. The film made on the life of Jackie Robinson[1]
B. Negro women in the news . . .
C. Increasing Job Opportunities for Negro Women . . .
D. Negro in International Relations . . .
E. National awards to Dr. Ralph Bunche[2]

From time to time VOA prepares features and interviews dealing with the American Negro. See the INTERVIEW with Gladys Watts . . . retiring president, Illinois Assn. of Negro Women. Also, INTERVIEW with Eunice Carter, UN Observer for National Council of Negro Women . . . When the Howard University[3] players visited Europe, VOA interviewed the group both when it left the country and when it returned.

<u>The Negro and Politics</u> – Although the United States is under steady attack by Moscow on the status of the American Negro, VOA has not attempted to answer these specifically, but wherever possible does report the progress of the Negro in different areas in American life. For example, the attached series of six scripts on SEGREGATION AND THE LAW, based on the Supreme Court decision on Negro Civil rights.[4]

VOA has also carried statements made by prominent American Negroes and Negro organizations on Communism. This was true, for instance, of the reaction of American Negro leaders, such as Walter White, Rev. Adam Clayton

---

[1] Jackie Robinson was the first African American baseball player to be admitted to the Major League. Starting in 1947, he played for the Brooklyn Dodgers.

[2] Ralph Bunche was a prominent African American scholar and diplomat. In 1950, he received the Nobel Peace Prize for helping to ease conflict in the Middle East resulting from the creation of the nation of Israel.

[3] A historically black university in Washington, D.C.

[4] The specific case is not mentioned. This may be a reference to *Sweatt v. Painter* (1950), in which the Supreme Court ruled that Texas had violated the equal protection clause of the 14th Amendment by creating a separate law school for African Americans; or a reference to *McLaurin v. Oklahoma State Regents* (1950), in which the Supreme Court also ruled against a state's specific practices of racial segregation at a state university.

Powell (Member of Congress) and Dr. Max Yergan to various pro-Soviet statements by Paul Robeson.[5] Note the attached script reviewing William A. Nolan's book COMMUNISM VERSUS THE NEGRO.

It should be pointed out, at the same time, that VOA does not avoid mentioning those tragic instances which periodically take place in some American communities because of bitter race feeling. It has always been VOA's policy to carry news of race riots and lynchings when these unhappily occur. However, VOA also endeavors to place these developments in proper focus, so far as overseas listeners are concerned, by reporting the efforts of law and order to bring the perpetrators of these injustices to book.

The Negro and Art – Naturally VOA has done a great deal with American Negro culture. This has not only involved reviewing the work of such prominent Negro writers as Richard Wright and others, but also the broadcasting of songs by such Negro artists as Marian Anderson and Dorothy Maynor.[6] In these instances, VOA does not necessarily call attention to the race of the artist used. In fact, as a general policy, VOA refers to individuals as Negroes only when this is essential for purposes of clarity.

---

[5] All of these men were African Americans. Actor and singer Paul Robeson was openly supportive of communism. His public criticism of U.S. Cold War policies led to his passport being revoked in 1950 and to his surveillance by the FBI. (The Supreme Court later ruled that the State Department had violated Robeson's rights by taking his passport.) Walter White was a leader of the NAACP, the National Association for the Advancement of Colored People. Adam Clayton Powell was a prominent New York City minister and a Democratic member of Congress. Dr. Max Yergan, a civil rights activist, had previously supported communism but, by 1952, he had become a fierce critic of communism. All three men had recently denounced Robeson's political views.

[6] Marian Anderson and Dorothy Maynor were both singers.

Document 12

"A Policy of Boldness"
John Foster Dulles
May 19, 1952

John Foster Dulles served as Dwight D. Eisenhower's Secretary of State from 1953 – 1959. Dulles had decades of foreign policy experience before joining the Eisenhower administration. As a young man he served as an economic advisor during the Paris Peace Proceedings in 1919. (His uncle Robert Lansing was Woodrow Wilson's Secretary of State.) An attorney during the interwar years, Dulles specialized in issues of international law, business, and finance. Firmly anti-communist, he supported early U.S. Cold War policies, including the Marshall Plan (Document 3). As this article shows, however, he was critical of the Truman administration's implementation of these policies.

Dulles's call for a "policy of boldness" is significant for two primary reasons. First, the policy became part of the Republican Party's 1952 platform, which condemned containment as a "negative, futile, and immoral policy" that "abandons countless human beings to a despotism and godless terrorism." Republicans promised to implement a foreign policy that would free captive people from communism's grip. Second, Dulles's recommendations heavily influenced the Eisenhower administration's so-called New Look, officially known as the Basic National Security Policy. The New Look rejected some of the premises of NSC 68, the foundational security policy of the Truman administration starting in 1950 (Document 6). To reduce the costs of large standing military forces, the United States would rely on its superior nuclear arsenal to deter communist aggression. The New Look was based upon the United States' existing and projected advantages in the technology of modern warfare, especially airpower, missiles, and nuclear weapons. The New Look also called for intensified psychological warfare programs, expanded intelligence-gathering, and covert operations.

Source: John Foster Dulles, "A Policy of Boldness," Life, Vol. 32, no. 20 (May 19, 1952), 146-57.

Soviet Communism confronts our nation with its gravest peril. To meet its long-term strategy of encirclement and strangulation, we have adopted a series of emergency measures which are fantastically costly not only in money but in their warping of our American way of life.

No one would begrudge the cost of what we are doing if, in fact, it was adequate and was ending the peril, and if there was no better way. Actually, our policies are *inadequate* in scope. They are *not* ending the peril. There is a better way.

The costs of our present policies are perilously high in money, in freedom and in friendships.

The Administration's "security policies" would this year cost us, in money, about 60 billion, of which about 99% goes for military purposes and for equipment (which will quickly become obsolete and demand replacement indefinitely). Such gigantic expenditures unbalance our budget and require taxes so heavy that they discourage incentive. They so cheapen the dollar that savings, pensions and Social Security reserves have already lost much of their value.

What is worse, this concentration on military matters is – to use George Washington's words – "inauspicious to liberty."[1] It leads to encroachments on civil rights and transfers from the civilian to the military decisions which profoundly affect our domestic life and our foreign relations.

We are also rapidly expending our friendships and prestige in the world. Increasing numbers turn away from our policies as too militaristic, too costly, too erratic and too inconclusive for them to follow. Our far-flung, extravagant and surreptitious military projects are frightening many who feel that we are conducting a private feud with Russia, which may endanger them, rather than performing a public service for peace....

Our present negative policies will never end the type of sustained offensive which Soviet Communism is mounting; they will never end the peril nor bring relief from the exertions which devour our economic, political and moral vitals. Ours are treadmill policies which, at best, might perhaps keep us in the same place until we drop exhausted....

Where do we go from here? ...

Looked at in any impartial way, we are the world's greatest and strongest power. The only commodity in which we seem deficient is faith. In all material things we have a productivity far exceeding that of Russia: our steel production is about three and one half times that of the Soviet Union, and in aluminum, petroleum and electric power our superiority is even greater. Our people have a standard of education, an inventive talent and a technical skill unmatched by any of the peoples under Soviet rule.

On the Soviet side a dozen people in the Kremlin are attempting to rule 800 million human beings – while trying to conquer more. All except a privileged

---

[1] The quote is from George Washington's 1796 farewell address.

few work under conditions which sternly deny them the "pursuit of happiness." Within Russia itself the discontent can be judged by the 15 million prisoners in forced labor camps – more than twice the membership of the Soviet Communist party. Even the leaders are suspicious of each other as each wonders whether the other plots his purge. . . .

The free should not be numbed by the sight of this vast graveyard of human liberties. It is the despots who should feel haunted. They, not we, should fear the future.

As we stop fretting and start thinking, the first problem to tackle is the strictly military one. It comes in the form of a paradox: for we must seek a military formula more effective than any devised to date – that we may no longer be so overridingly preoccupied with purely military necessity.

The dimensions of the problem are plain: at least 3,000,000 Soviet soldiers regularly under arms, another 3,000,000 to 4,000,000 in the Chinese Red armies. These forces, poised in a central area could strike with massive power east, south or west at any one of more than 20 nations along the 20,000-mile boundary which runs from near Alaska down by Japan, through East Asia and South Asia, along the Middle and Near East to Europe and up through Central Europe to the North Cape. . . .

Those who think only of Western Europe and of making it "impregnable" – without regard to the Near, Middle and Far East and Africa – are just as blind as those who think only of the United States and of making it "impregnable." Policies that do not defend freedom in Asia are fatally defective.

How do we defend it? Obviously, we cannot build a 20,000-mile Maginot Line[2] or match the Red armies, man for man, gun for gun and tank for tank at any particular time or place their general staff selects. To attempt that would mean real strength nowhere and bankruptcy everywhere.

There is one solution and only one: that is for the free world to develop the will and organize the means to retaliate instantly against open aggression by Red armies, so that, if it occurred anywhere, we could and would strike back where it hurts, by means of our choosing.

The principle involved is as simple as that of our municipal police forces. We do not station armed guards at every house to stop aggressors – that would be economic suicide – but we deter potential aggressors by making it probable that if they aggress, they will lose in punishment more than they can gain by aggression. . . .

---

[2] The Maginot Line, a series of fortifications, was built by France at great expense after World War I to protect the nation from a German attack. The failure of the Maginot Line to prevent a German conquest during World War II made it a metaphor for costly, ineffective military measures.

Today atomic energy, coupled with strategic air and sea power, provides the community of free nations with vast new possibilities of organizing a community power to stop open aggression before it starts and reduce, to the vanishing point, the risk of general war. So far these weapons are merely part of national arsenals for use in fighting general war when it has come. If that catastrophe occurs, it will be because we have allowed these new and awesome forces to become the ordinary killing tools of the soldier when, in the hands of the statesmen, they could serve as effective political weapons in defense of the peace. . . .

. . . New methods of defense are needed to save the free nations from the dilemma, which present policies impose, of choosing between murder from without or suicide from within.

That is the enlightened and effective way to proceed. It is a way that we can afford to live with, and until there is effective international disarmament, it is the way we cannot afford to live without.

Once the free world has established a military defense, it can undertake what has been too long delayed – a political offense. . . .

. . . We should be *dynamic*, we should use *ideas* as weapons; and these ideas should conform to *moral* principles. . . .

. . . [L]iberation from the yoke of Moscow will not occur for a very long time, and courage in neighboring lands will not be sustained, *unless the United States makes it publicly known that it wants and expects liberation to occur.* The mere statement of that wish and expectation would change, in an electrifying way, the mood of the captive peoples. It would put heavy new burdens on the jailers and create new opportunities for liberation.

Here are some specific acts which we could take:

1) We could make it clear, on the highest authority of the President and the Congress, that U.S. policy seeks as one of its peaceful goals the eventual restoration of genuine independence in the nations of Europe and Asia now dominated by Moscow, and that we will not be a party to any "deal" confirming the rule of Soviet despotism over the alien people which it now dominates.

2) We could welcome the creation in the free world of political "task forces" to develop a freedom program for each of the captive nations. Each group would be made up of those who are proved patriots, who have practical resourcefulness and who command confidence and respect at home and abroad.

3) We could stimulate the escape from behind the Iron Curtain[3] of those who can help to develop these programs.

---

[3] Popularized by Winston Churchill in a 1946 speech, the phrase "iron curtain" refers to the border between democratic and communist nations in Europe.

4) The activities of the Voice of America and such private committees as those for Free Europe and Free Asia could be coordinated with these freedom programs. The agencies would be far more effective if given concrete jobs to do.

5) We could coordinate our economic, commercial and cultural relations with the freedom programs, cutting off or licensing intercourse as seemed most effective from time to time.

6) We could end diplomatic relations with present governments which are in fact only puppets of Moscow, if and when that would promote the freedom programs.

7) We could seek to bring other free nations to unite with us in proclaiming, in a great new Declaration of Independence, our policies toward the captive nations.

We do not want a series of bloody uprisings and reprisals . . . But we can know, for history proves, that the spirit of patriotism burns unquenched in Poles, Czechs, Hungarians, Romanians, Bulgarians, Chinese and others, and we can be confident that within two, five or 10 years substantial parts of the present captive world can peacefully regain national independence. That will mark the beginning of the end of Soviet despotism's attempt at world conquest. . . .

Document 13

Organized Evacuation of Civilian Populations in Civil Defense

Federal Civil Defense Administration

June 12, 1952

The United States used atomic weapons to end the war with Japan in the summer of 1945. The Soviet Union tested its first atomic weapon in August 1949, sooner than anticipated by U.S. national security experts. (Communist espionage during World War II aided the Soviets' acquisition of nuclear technology; Document 10.) The continental United States was untouched by the strategic bombing that devastated much of Europe and Japan during the war, but nuclear weapons erased Americans' sense of security. In its report on the effects of the atomic bombing of Hiroshima and Nagasaki, the U.S. Strategic Bombing Survey ominously remarked, "The Survey's investigators, as they proceeded about their study, found an insistent question framing itself in their minds: 'What if the target for the bomb had been an American City?'"

Starting in the late 1940s, the U.S. federal government carried out a national program to educate civilians about the threat of nuclear weapons and to provide advice on how citizens might protect themselves. The Korean War (Documents 8–9) especially raised fears about an attack on the United States, leading to the establishment of the Federal Civil Defense Administration (FCDA) in 1951. The FCDA and successor agencies were based upon the concept of self-help: the federal government would provide data, policy, and promotional materials, but the responsibility for preparing for nuclear war lay with states, cities, and individuals. However, the enormous loss of life and physical devastation that nuclear war would surely bring raised serious questions about such an approach. As a congressional subcommittee put it, "Self-help cannot provide nation-wide protection against the deadly effects of exploding nuclear bombs any more than self-help can build the bombs." Perhaps recognizing the difficulty of effective civil defense, few Americans paid attention to it throughout the Cold War.

This document exposes the steep challenges of preparing the home front for nuclear war. The FCDA subsequently changed its evacuation policy more than once. Such reversals only intensified the question at the heart of civil defense: was it possible to prepare citizens for nuclear war by only using plans, guidance, and consultation?

Source: Papers of Harry S. Truman, President's Secretary's Files, National Security Files, box 217, folder "Meeting 119, June 18, 1952," Harry S. Truman Presidential Library, Independence, MO.

Federal Civil Defense Administration
Washington 15, D.C.

SUBJECT: ORGANIZED EVACUATION OF CIVILIAN POPULATIONS IN CIVIL DEFENSE

I. Purpose

This statement establishes the policy of the Federal Civil Defense Administration regarding the evacuation of civilians threatened or affected by enemy attack.

II. Definition

Evacuation in civil defense is the organized, timed, and supervised movement of a portion of the civilians from an area authoritatively designated as dangerous or otherwise critical, and their reception and care in more suitable areas.

III. Policy

It is the policy of the Federal Civil Defense Administration to:

A. Develop national plans and programs which will assure uniformity of planning by the several States for evacuation, where appropriate and necessary.

B. Consult with the several States with a view to their designating specific areas for which evacuation plans should be prepared, and aid them in the selection of reception areas, where appropriate.

C. Sponsor and furnish advice, support, and assistance to the States in:

1. Prompt development of uniform State and local plans for evacuation and reception areas.

2. Implementation of evacuation by regional State, and local civil defense authorities.

3. Coordination of all evacuation plans with national and regional civil defense planning and with planning of appropriate military authorities.

D. Recommend to the several States that they base their plans for the evacuation of civilian populations only on the following:

1. <u>Pre-attack</u>: no evacuation from any area prior to an enemy attack on that area.
2. <u>During attack</u>: no evacuation from an area while under attack.
3. <u>Post-attack</u>:
   a. When evacuation is the sole method available for adequately minimizing the effects of enemy attack.
   b. When evacuation is restricted to priority groups specified or recognized by appropriate civil defense authorities.
   c. When evacuation is under the direction of constituted state or local civil defense officials.

IV.　<u>Authority</u>

Section 3(b) of Public Law 920, 81st Congress, defines the term "civil defense" as including " . . . measures to be taken in preparation for anticipated attack (including . . . when appropriate, the non-military evacuation of civil population):" "measures to be taken during attack (including . . . the evacuation of personnel to shelter areas..." "measures to be taken following attack (including . . . emergency welfare measures; . . . " Section 201 (a) authorized the Administrator to prepare national plans and programs for the civil defense of the United States and to sponsor and direct such plans and programs.

V.　<u>Effective Date</u>

This policy is effective as of the date of issuance.

Document 14

Farewell Address

President Harry S. Truman

January 15, 1953

Harry S. Truman's popularity was at a record low when he delivered his Farewell Address in early 1953 from the White House. The status of the Cold War was a major reason for the outgoing president's low approval rating. Although Truman was the primary architect of U.S. Cold War policies (Documents 2–4 and 6), the stalemated war in Korea (Documents 8–9) and Republican calls to replace containment with a "policy of boldness" (Document 12) had taken their toll.

Shrugging off the criticism, Truman called on all citizens to support the new president, Republican Dwight D. Eisenhower. He also reviewed the many actions his administration had taken to contain communism: aid to Greece and Turkey, the Marshall Plan, the North Atlantic Treaty Organization, and defense of South Korea (Documents 2–3 and 8.) As a Cold War document, the speech is much more than a review of the conflict's first eight years. Truman also expressed his belief that the United States and its allies would ultimately prevail. "I have a deep and abiding faith in the destiny of free men. With patience and courage, we shall some day move on into a new era."

Truman's prediction proved to be accurate. The Cold War's finish did, in fact, result from "trouble in the satellite states" that caused a change in the way that the Soviet leadership thought about Eastern Europe. This "change inside the Kremlin" spurred further democratization efforts, helping to bring down the Iron Curtain. Although Truman did not live to see the end of the Cold War, he forecast it.

Source: Public Papers of the Presidents of the United States: Harry S. Truman, 1952-1953 *(Washington, D.C.: U.S. Government Printing Office, 1966), 1197-1202. Available at https://goo.gl/tMr2BL.*

My fellow Americans:

I am happy to have this opportunity to talk to you once more before I leave the White House.

. . . I have no new revelations to make – no political statements – no policy announcements. There are simply a few things in my heart that I want to say to you. I want to say "goodby" and "thanks for your help." And I want to talk to you a little while about what has happened since I became your President. . . .

I want all of you to realize how big a job, how hard a job, it is – not for my sake, because I am stepping out of it – but for the sake of my successor.[1] He needs the understanding and the help of every citizen. It is not enough for you to come out once every 4 years and vote for a candidate, and then go back home and say, "Well, I've done my part, now let the new President do the worrying." He can't do the job alone.

Regardless of your politics, whether you are Republican or Democrat, your fate is tied up with what is done here in this room. The President is President of the whole country. We must give him our support as citizens of the United States. He will have mine, and I want you to give him yours.

I suppose that history will remember my term in office as the years when the "cold war" began to overshadow our lives. I have had hardly a day in office that has not been dominated by this all-embracing struggle – this conflict between those who love freedom and those who would lead the world back into slavery and darkness. And always in the background there has been the atomic bomb.

But when history says that my term of office saw the beginning of the cold war, it will also say that in those 8 years we have set the course that can win it. We have succeeded in carving out a new set of policies to attain peace – positive policies, policies of world leadership, policies that express faith in other free people. We have averted world war III up to now, and we may already have succeeded in establishing conditions which can keep that war from happening as far ahead as man can see. . . .

. . . [I]n early 1947, the Soviet Union threatened Greece and Turkey. The British sent me a message saying they could no longer keep their forces in that area. Something had to be done at once, or the eastern Mediterranean would be taken over by the Communists. On March 12th, I went before the Congress and stated our determination to help the people of Greece and Turkey maintain their independence. Today, Greece is still free and independent; and Turkey is a bulwark of strength at a strategic corner of the world.

Then came the Marshall plan which saved Europe, the heroic Berlin airlift,[2] and our military aid programs. . . .

---

[1] Dwight D. Eisenhower.

[2] The Berlin airlift (June 26, 1948 – September 30, 1949) was the supply of food and fuel to Berlin by Allied air forces after the Soviets cut off rail and road access to the city, which was within their zone of control but shared by the Allied powers, in a dispute over the use of the West German Deutsche mark in the city. The airlift succeeded; the Soviets reopened access to the city.

Most important of all, we acted in Korea. . . .

. . . If we let the Republic of Korea go under, some other country would be next, and then another. And all the time, the courage and confidence of the free world would be ebbing away, just as it did in the 1930's. . . .[3]

As I have thought about our worldwide struggle with the Communists these past 8 years – day in and day out – I have never once doubted that you, the people of our country, have the will to do what is necessary to win this terrible fight against communism. . . .

Then, some of you may ask, when and how will the cold war end? I think I can answer that simply. The Communist world has great resources, and it looks strong. But there is a fatal flaw in their society. Theirs is a godless system, a system of slavery; there is no freedom in it, no consent. The Iron Curtain, the secret police, the constant purges, all these are symptoms of a great basic weakness – the rulers' fear of their own people.

In the long run the strength of our free society, and our ideals, will prevail over a system that has respect for neither God nor man.

Last week, in my State of the Union Message to the Congress – and I hope you will all take the time to read it – I explained how I think we will finally win through.

As the free world grows stronger, more united, more attractive to men on both sides of the Iron Curtain – and as the Soviet hopes for easy expansion are blocked – then there will have to come a time of change in the Soviet world. Nobody can say for sure when that is going to be, or exactly how it will come about, whether by revolution, or trouble in the satellite states, or by a change inside the Kremlin.

Whether the Communist rulers shift their policies of their own free will – or whether the change comes about in some other way – I have not a doubt in the world that a change will occur.

I have a deep and abiding faith in the destiny of free men. With patience and courage, we shall some day move on into a new era – a wonderful golden age – an age when we can use the peaceful tools that science has forged for us to do away with poverty and human misery everywhere on earth. . . .

And now, the time has come for me to say good night – and God bless you all.

---

[3] The fear of one country after another falling to communism was popularly called the domino theory, after a game based on vertical tiles that fall in succession.

Document 15

Testimony before the House Committee on Un-American Activities

Robert E. Treuhaft

December 3, 1953

The House Committee on Un-American Activities (commonly called the House Un-American Activities Committee or HUAC) had its origins in a special committee organized in the mid-1930s to investigate fascist activity in the United States. By the late 1930s, the committee had also begun investigating domestic communism, looking for links between members of the Communist Party of the United States of America (CPUSA) and New Deal agencies such as the Federal Theater Project. The Cold War gave the committee renewed purpose, and it became a permanent committee in 1945. HUAC's 1947 investigation of communist influence in Hollywood attracted national attention and controversy. Ten screenwriters refused to answer questions; all ten were charged with contempt. (Nine were secret party members, but membership in the CPUSA was not a crime.)

Subsequent HUAC hearings investigated Soviet espionage, communist ideas and practices, and alleged communist influence in student organizations, the media, and, as seen in the following document, labor unions. By 1953, U.S. labor unions had taken many steps to prove they were anti-communist; the Congress of Industrial Organizations, for example, expelled numerous unions for communist connections between 1948 and 1950. Concerns about radicalism within the labor unions continued, though critics charged HUAC with masking an attack on all organized labor in the name of anti-communism.

Robert E. Treuhaft was one of two attorneys who represented a San Francisco local of a warehouse union. His statement before the HUAC is significant for showing the fear generated by subversive investigations, the already established use in 1953 of "McCarthyism" (Documents 5 and 7) as a polemical device, and the partisan divide on the issue of how to respond to Cold War security concerns.

Source: U.S. Congress, House, Committee on Un-American Activities, Investigation of Communist Activities in the San Francisco Area – Part 3, 83rd Congress, 1st sess., December 3 1953, 3329-41. Available at https://goo.gl/nxX6q5

Mr. TREUHAFT: I am obliged to appear before this committee without assistance of counsel, Mr. Tavenner,[1] because of the fact that the repressive activities of this committee have made it impossible for me to secure the assistance of attorneys of my choice. This is a serious charge for a lawyer to make. I am compelled, however, to make it because the state of affairs that I have found to exist in this regard is truly shocking.

A month ago I received a subpoena[2] calling for my appearance before this committee. My law partner and I have been, for many years, and are now, general counsel for the East Bay Division of Warehouse Union Local 6, ILWU,[3] a labor organization which is one of the principal targets under attack by this committee. In fact, I am sure this was well known to the committee's investigators, and I cannot down the suspicion that my representation of this union had something to do with the fact that my law partner and I are the only East Bay[4] lawyers subpoenaed before the committee at these hearings so far as I know.

I readily agreed to represent four East Bay members of this union as their attorney, who likewise were subpoenaed, despite the fact that I, myself, had been subpoenaed as a witness.

Upon receipt of my subpoena I immediately began to make diligent efforts to secure counsel to represent me. I compiled a list of the 7 leading East Bay lawyers whom I would want to represent me because of their known ability in their profession and because all of them had, from time to time, shown themselves to be champions of the right of advocacy. All had a sound understanding of due process of law and of the other constitutional rights and immunities which are daily trampled upon by this committee. . . .

The first lawyer, whom I will call lawyer No. 1, holds high office in the Alameda County Bar Association. When I first approached this lawyer, he told me that he could see no reason why he could not represent me. The next day, however, he informed me that he felt that he could not do so because of the controversial nature and the publicity attendant upon hearings before this committee and because of his position in the county bar association.

The second lawyer I consulted out of this list, lawyer No. 2, is a former judge who has an active practice on both sides of the bay. I discussed with him the position which I intended to take before this committee; that is, to uphold the Constitution and to rely upon the first and fifth amendments to the

---

[1] Frank S. Tavenner, counsel to HUAC.

[2] A subpoena is a legal order requiring someone to appear in court or, in this case, before Congress.

[3] International Longshoremen's and Warehousemen's Union.

[4] Of the San Francisco area.

Constitution as they might apply to every question that this committee might put to me.

This attorney, who is highly placed in the bar, agreed fully with me in principle and stated that it was his opinion that my decision was sound and wise. He told me that he would like to represent me.

After conferring with his associate, however, he called me in again, and he said that he was very sorry that he could not because representing me with the attendant publicity or representing any witness before this committee would involve financial hardship. . . .

The third lawyer I went to see and offered a retainer to represent me before these hearings was an older lawyer, and he was a better financially established lawyer . . . [but] he told me, "Try to find a younger lawyer. The activities before this committee would be too strenuous," he thought, the publicity would be harmful.

The fourth lawyer I went to is a leading criminal lawyer in the East Bay. We have been on very friendly terms, and he readily agreed to represent me without any hesitation at all . . . [but] 3 days before I was supposed to come here, he called me, and he told me that his partner had just returned from out of town and had learned that he had undertaken to represent me. He said that his partner represented a bank, and that his partner felt that the attendant publicity would be so harmful to them that he insisted that they could not represent a witness before this committee. He told me this with very personal regret. He also expressed the view – his partner did – that any attorney who represented a witness before this committee might find himself in a position where he was persecuted by other governmental agencies . . .

. . . [A]ll of these lawyers that I named had real courage. I went to them because they were courageous. I am not condemning nor criticizing the lawyers. I am condemning this committee for trying its cases in the newspapers and over the radio. I am condemning this committee for depriving me of right of counsel by its slanderous attacks, attacks by inference, which even repel and revolt some of the Democratic members of this committee . . .

Now, the canon of ethics of the American Bar Association, as I think Representative Moulder[5] has referred to, states, and this is law for lawyers, that no lawyer shall, for reasons personal to himself, reject any cause because it is unpopular. All of the lawyers that I consulted did reject this cause for reasons personal to themselves, but for reasons created by the hysteria engendered by this committee in the public mind, the fear that anybody who appears before

---

[5] Morgan M. Moulder, a Democratic Congressman from Missouri and a member of HUAC.

this committee is labeled as a spy or something subversive, and that the taint may rub off onto the lawyer. . . .

. . . This whole situation is McCarthyism. President Truman recently described it as such. He said that it is the use of the big lie and the unfounded accusation against any citizen in the name of Americanism – in quotes – and security – in quotes. It is the use of the power of the demagogue who lives on untruth, and I am reading here, Mr. Jackson,[6] because I am quoting, and I don't want to be inaccurate:

"It is the spread of fear," President Truman said, "and the destruction of faith at every level of our society. This horrible cancer," he said, "is eating at the vitals of America, and it can destroy the great edifice of freedom."[7]

Mr. Truman went on to say that this situation should serve to alert the people to the terrible danger that our Nation and each citizen faces and urge his fellow countrymen to "be aroused and fight this evil at every level of our national life."

I am prepared to fight this evil at every level, and I intend to ask the State bar to look into a situation which I think is truly disgraceful, where lawyers with real courage and standing are afraid to come forward and represent clients before this committee. . . .

---

[6] Donald L. Jackson, a Republican Congressman from California and a member of HUAC.

[7] Treuhaft quotes from a speech former president Truman gave in Independence, Missouri, November 17, 1953. *The Chicago Tribune* printed the speech, November 17, 1953, Part 1, p. 5. The text is available online at https://goo.gl/DXadFk.

Document 16

National Security Council Directive, NSC 5412/2, Covert Operations
December 28, 1955

Covert or secret operations were a major part of the Cold War, and the United States, the Soviet Union, and their respective allies were frequent sponsors of these efforts. The United States had already undertaken numerous and successful covert operations prior to this directive, most notably in Iran (1953) and Guatemala (1954). In both these nations, U.S. covert actions helped install pro-American governments. As this document makes clear, the National Security Council was also responding to the growing number of aggressive, secret communist operations threatening the United States and its allies.

The purposes of American-led covert operations included discrediting communism, increasing the attraction of U.S. policies and values, and building up hidden networks of anti-communist operatives within communist states. The directive authorized the Central Intelligence Agency to plan and execute the operations. The definition of "covert operations" was broad, covering sabotage, propaganda, and political action, among many other activities. As the directive indicates, whatever the action, it was supposed to be conducted in ways to conceal the involvement of the United States or, if such connections were uncovered, to allow the United States to plausibly deny them.

For examples of subsequent covert operations, see Documents 24, 35, 38, and 39.

Source: National Security Council Directive, NSC 5412/2, December 28, 1955 [Document 250], The Foreign Relations of the United States, 1950 – 1955, The Intelligence Community, 1950-1955 (Washington, D.C.: U.S. Government Printing Office, 2007).

National Security Council Directive
COVERT OPERATIONS

The National Security Council, taking cognizance of the vicious covert activities of the USSR and Communist China and the governments, parties and groups dominated by them, (hereinafter collectively referred to as "International Communism") to discredit and defeat the aims and activities of the United States and other powers of the free world, determined . . . that, in the interests of world peace and U.S. national security, the overt foreign activities of the U.S. Government should be supplemented by covert operations.

The Central Intelligence Agency had already been charged by the National Security Council with conducting espionage and counterespionage operations abroad. It therefore seemed desirable, for operational reasons, not to create a new agency for covert operations, but, subject to directives from the NSC, to place the responsibility for them on the Central Intelligence Agency and correlate them with espionage and counter-espionage operations under the over-all control of the Director of Central Intelligence.

The NSC has determined that such covert operations shall to the greatest extent practicable, in the light of U.S. and Soviet capabilities and taking into account the risk of war, be designed to:

- Create and exploit troublesome problems for International Communism, impair relations between the USSR and Communist China and between them and their satellites, complicate control within the USSR, Communist China and their satellites, and retard the growth of the military and economic potential of the Soviet bloc.
- Discredit the prestige and ideology of International Communism, and reduce the strength of its parties and other elements.
- Counter any threat of a party or individuals directly or indirectly responsive to Communist control to achieve dominant power in a free world country.
- Reduce International Communist control over any areas of the world.
- Strengthen the orientation toward the United States of the peoples and nations of the free world, accentuate, wherever possible, the identity of interest between such peoples and nations and the United States as well as favoring, where appropriate, those groups genuinely advocating or believing in the advancement of such mutual interests, and increase the capacity and will of such peoples and nations to resist International Communism.
- In accordance with established policies and to the extent practicable in areas dominated or threatened by International Communism, develop underground resistance and facilitate covert and guerrilla operations and ensure availability of those forces in the event of war, including wherever practicable provision of a base upon which the military may expand these forces in time of war within active theaters of operations as well as provision for stay-behind assets and escape and evasion facilities.

Under the authority of . . . the National Security Act of 1947[1], the National Security Council hereby directs that the Director of Central Intelligence shall be responsible for:

- Ensuring, through designated representatives of the Secretary of State and of the Secretary of Defense, that covert operations are planned and conducted in a manner consistent with United States foreign and military policies and with overt activities, and consulting with and obtaining advice from the Operations Coordinating Board and other departments or agencies as appropriate.

- Informing, through appropriate channels and on a need-to-know basis, agencies of the U.S. Government, both at home and abroad (including diplomatic and military representatives), of such operations as will affect them.

In addition . . . , the following provisions shall apply to wartime covert operations:

- Plans for covert operations to be conducted in active theaters of war and any other areas in which U.S. forces are engaged in combat operations will be drawn up with the assistance of the Department of Defense and will be in consonance with and complementary to approved war plans of the Joint Chiefs of Staff.

- Covert operations in active theaters of war and any other areas in which U.S. forces are engaged in combat operations will be conducted under such command and control relationships as have been or may in the future be approved by the Department of Defense.

As used in this directive, "covert operations" shall be understood to be all activities conducted pursuant to this directive which are so planned and executed that any U.S. Government responsibility for them is not evident to unauthorized persons and that if uncovered the U.S. Government can plausibly disclaim any responsibility for them. Specifically, such operations shall include any covert activities related to: propaganda; political action; economic warfare; preventive direct action, including sabotage, anti-sabotage, demolition; escape and evasion and evacuation measures; subversion against hostile states or groups including assistance to underground resistance movements, guerrillas and refugee liberation groups; support of indigenous and anti-communist elements in threatened countries of the free world; deception plans and operations; and all activities compatible with this directive necessary to accomplish the foregoing. Such operations shall not include: armed conflict by

---

[1] The National Security Act of 1947 created the National Security Council and the Central Intelligence Agency.

recognized military forces, espionage and counterespionage, nor cover and deception for military operations.

Except as the President otherwise directs, designated representatives of the Secretary of State and of the Secretary of Defense of the rank of Assistant Secretary or above, and a representative of the President designated for this purpose, shall hereafter be advised in advance of major covert programs initiated by CIA under this policy or as otherwise directed, and shall be the normal channel for giving policy approval for such programs as well as for securing coordination of support therefor among the Departments of State and Defense and the CIA.

Document 17

Radio and Television Report to the American People on the Developments in Eastern Europe and the Middle East

President Dwight D. Eisenhower
October 31, 1956

In late October 1956, a revolt broke out against the government of Hungary, one of many Eastern European nations in which the Soviet Union had imposed communist regimes after World War II. Although Hungary was technically a sovereign state, its government ultimately answered to the Soviet Union. Hungary was also a member of the Warsaw Pact, an alliance of communist states headed by the Soviet Union. The rebels hoped to replace Hungary's communist government with a democratic, neutral regime. Such a change would have forced the Soviet Union to withdraw its military forces from Hungary. The threat of Soviet intervention in Hungary was high, but on October 31, the Soviet government made a surprising announcement: it was willing to negotiate about the stationing of its troops in Hungary.

In this radio and television address, President Eisenhower refers to the unexpected Soviet offer as a significant statement but also warned, "We cannot yet know if these avowed purposes will be truly carried out." He promised economic support to the Hungarian rebels and to those in other Eastern European countries who might take power from the Soviet Union. Such a commitment reflected the policy of the Eisenhower administration to not just contain communism, but also liberate people from its rule (Document 12). Many Hungarian rebels hoped the United States might directly aid the rebellion, but Eisenhower did not take, nor did he ever consider, such a step, which risked war with the Soviet Union in Europe.

On November 4, the Soviet Union suddenly ended its conciliatory stance and ordered its troops to crush the revolt. The Soviets feared looking weak and also worried that negotiation with the Hungarians might encourage revolt in other satellite states. A pro-Soviet government was reinstalled in Hungary. The U.S. decision to not aid the Hungarian rebels was pragmatic and prudent, given the risks of intervention, but the limited response also highlighted the difficulty of fulfilling the global liberation of captive people.

(The speech also explained the U.S. response to the Suez Canal crisis in the Middle East, which coincidentally occurred at the same time as the Hungarian

uprising. *Eisenhower denounced an armed attack on Egypt by France, Great Britain, and Israel; these three nations were trying to keep Egypt from controlling the Suez Canal. U.S condemnation of the attack, which failed to achieve its objective, showed the United States would not automatically support its allies in their efforts to hold onto imperial power. That portion of the speech has been omitted.)*

Source: Public Papers of the Presidents of the United States: Dwight D. Eisenhower, 1956 *(Washington, D.C.: U.S. Government Printing Office, 1958), 1060-6. Available at https://goo.gl/xyC23Z.*

My Fellow Americans:

Tonight I report to you as your President.

We all realize that the full and free debate of a political campaign surrounds us.[1] But the events and issues I wish to place before you this evening have no connection whatsoever with matters of partisanship. They are concerns of every American...

In Eastern Europe there is the dawning of a new day. It has not been short or easy in coming.

After World War II, the Soviet Union used military force to impose on the nations of Eastern Europe, governments of Soviet choice – servants of Moscow.

It has been consistent United States policy – without regard to political party – to seek to end this situation. We have sought to fulfill the wartime pledge of the United Nations that these countries, over-run by wartime armies, would once again know sovereignty and self-government.

We could not, of course, carry out this policy by resort to force. Such force would have been contrary both to the best interests of the Eastern European peoples and to the abiding principles of the United Nations. But we did help to keep alive the hope of these peoples for freedom.

Beyond this, they needed from us no education in the worth of national independence and personal liberty – for, at the time of the American Revolution, it was many of them who came to our land to aid our cause. Now, recently the pressure of the will of these peoples for national independence has become more and more insistent. . . .

. . . [A]ll the world has been watching dramatic events in Hungary where this brave people, as so often in the past, have offered their very lives for independence from foreign masters. Today, it appears, a new Hungary is rising

---

[1] The 1956 presidential election was taking place less than a week later, on November 6. Eisenhower's opponent was Democrat Adlai Stevenson, who also ran against Eisenhower in 1952.

from this struggle, a Hungary which we hope from our hearts will know full and free nationhood.

We have rejoiced in all these historic events.

Only yesterday the Soviet Union issued an important statement on its relations with all the countries of Eastern Europe. This statement recognized the need for review of Soviet policies, and the amendment of these policies to meet the demands of the people for greater national independence and personal freedom. The Soviet Union declared its readiness to consider the withdrawal of Soviet "advisers" – who have been, as you know, the effective ruling force in Soviet occupied countries – and also to consider withdrawal of Soviet forces from Poland, Hungary and Rumania.

We cannot yet know if these avowed purposes will be truly carried out.

But two things are clear.

First, the fervor and the sacrifice of the peoples of these countries, in the name of freedom, have themselves brought real promise that the light of liberty soon will shine again in this darkness.

And second, if the Soviet Union indeed faithfully acts upon its announced intention, the world will witness the greatest forward stride toward justice, trust and understanding among nations in our generation.

These are the facts. How has your government responded to them?

The United States has made clear its readiness to assist economically the new and independent governments of these countries. . . . We have also publicly declared that we do not demand of these governments their adoption of any particular form of society as a condition upon our economic assistance. Our one concern is that they be free – for their sake, and for freedom's sake.

We have also – with respect to the Soviet Union – sought clearly to remove any false fears that we would look upon new governments in these Eastern European countries as potential military allies. We have no such ulterior purpose. We see these peoples as friends, and we wish simply that they be friends who are free. . . .

Document 18

The Kitchen Debate
Richard Nixon and Nikita Khrushchev
July 25, 1959

In the summer of 1959, Vice President Richard Nixon traveled to Moscow to formally open the American National Exhibit, a fair sponsored by the United States to show the Soviet people how Americans lived. Soviet Premier Nikita Khrushchev accompanied Nixon on a tour of the exhibit, with a team of journalists and photographers trailing them. The so-called Kitchen Debate was actually an unscripted series of exchanges between the two leaders about the merits and flaws of their respective economies and political systems. (One exchange came during a visit to the model American kitchen featured in the exhibit.)

Nixon and Khrushchev remained in good spirits as they argued; both leaders were mindful that their conversation was being captured using the new technology of color television and video recording. For Nixon, the encounter offered an opportunity to praise American technology, capitalism, and the high standard of living in the U.S. He observed that the debate itself showed the power and importance of free expression. For Khrushchev, the exchange allowed him to question how advanced the United States really was and to praise the communist system. The international attention the Kitchen Debate received showed the significant role that ideas and communication played in the Cold War.

Source: There is no complete record of all of Nixon and Khrushchev's conversations, and versions vary. The first excerpt below is a transcription from a CSPAN video of the conversation between Nixon and Khrushchev when they met to attend the exhibit; Richard Nixon and Nikita Khrushchev, "Kitchen Debate," July 24, 1959, CSPAN. Available at https://goo.gl/i4SCP5. The second, shorter excerpt is from "The Two Worlds: A Day-Long Debate," New York Times, July 25, 1959, 1, 3.

Interviewer: Tell us your general impressions of the exhibits.

Khrushchev: In speaking about impressions, it is now obvious that the builders haven't managed to complete their construction and the exhibits are not yet in place. Therefore, it is hard to comment, because what we see is the construction process rather than the exhibits we'd like to see. But I think that everything will be in place in a few hours and it will be a good exhibition.

Regarding our wishes, we wish America the very best to show its goods, products, and abilities, great abilities and we will gladly look and learn. Not only will we learn, but we also can show and do show you what we do. This will contribute to improved relations between our countries and among all countries to ensure peace throughout the world. We want only to live in peace and friendship with Americans because we are the most powerful nations. If we are friends then other countries will be friends. If someone tries to be a little bellicose then we can tug his ear a little and we can say "Don't you dare!" We can't be at war. These are times of nuclear weapons. A fool may start this war and a wise man won't be able to end that war. Hence, these are our guiding principles in policy, domestic and international. We wish you success in demonstrating America's capabilities and then we will be impressed. How long has America existed? Is it 300 years?

Unknown third party: 150 years of independence.

Khrushchev: Then we'll say America has existed 150 years and here is its level. We have existed almost 42 years and in another 7 years we will be on the same level as America. And then we'll move on ahead. When we pass you along the way we'll greet you amicably like this. [Khrushchev waves his hand.] Then if you like, we can stop and invite you to catch up. The question of social structure and well-being – you want to do that under capitalism? Well, you live as you wish. It's your business. That's a domestic issue and it doesn't concern us. We can feel sorry for you because you don't understand. Well then, live as you like. I'd like to say what is most important today. We are happy that the Vice President Mr. Nixon has arrived in Moscow for the opening of the exhibition. I personally express gratitude and on my colleagues' behalf, that Mr. President has sent me a message, which I haven't read yet, but I believe in advance that he sends warm wishes. I express gratitude to the messenger, and I hope you enjoy your visit . . . .

Interviewer: Mr. Vice President, from what you have seen of our exhibition how do you think it's going to impress the people here of the Soviet Union?

Nixon: Well I have not had much of an opportunity to see it yet, but I've seen a great number of photographers, as of course has the president and the prime minister. I think though that from what I have seen it's a very effective exhibit, and it's one that will cause a great deal of interest. I might say that this morning I . . . went down to visit a market . . . where the farmers from various outskirts of the city bring in their items to sell. As I was talking to them some of them came up to me and asked where they could get tickets to see the exhibition. I didn't have any with me at the time, but I made arrangements to have some sent down to the manager of the market. I can only say that there was a great deal of interest among these people who were workers and farmers et cetera. I would imagine that the exhibition from that standpoint will therefore be a considerable success. As far as Mr. Khrushchev's comments just now, they are in the tradition we learned to expect from him of speaking extemporaneously and frankly whenever he has an opportunity. And I'm glad that he did so on our color television at such a time as this. Of course later on we will both have the opportunity to speak later this evening and consequently I will not comment on the various subjects he raised at this point, except to say this. This, Mr. Khrushchev is one of the most advanced developments in communication that we have, at least, in our country. It is color television, of course. It is, as you will see in a few minutes, when you will see the tape of your speech and my comments in a few minutes, it is one of the best means of communication that has been developed and I can only say that if this competition that you have thus described so effectively, in which you plan to outstrip us, particularly in the production of consumer goods, if this competition is to do the best for our people, and for people everywhere, there must be a free exchange of ideas. There are some instances where you may be ahead of us, for example in the development of the thrust of your rockets for the exploration of outer space. There may be other areas, such as in color television, where we are ahead of you. In order for both of our peoples to. . .

Khrushchev: What do you mean, ahead? No, never. We've beaten you in rockets and in this technology we're ahead of you too.

Nixon: Wait until you see the picture.

Khrushchev: Good!

Interviewer: It will be interesting for you to know that this program is being recorded on Ampex color tape and it can be played back immediately, and you can't tell it isn't a live program.

Khrushchev: Soviet engineers [who] came were impressed by what they saw. I also join the awe of our Soviet engineers. The fact that Americans are smart people is something we've always believed and known because foolish people couldn't raise the economy to the level they have achieved. But we too are not fools swatting at flies with our nostrils. In forty-two years we have taken such a step! We're worthy partners! So, let's compete! Let's compete! Who can produce the most goods for the people, that system is better and it will win.

Nixon: Good. Let's have far more communication and exchange in this area that you speak of. We should hear you far more on our television. You should hear us far more on yours.

Khrushchev: Let's do it this way. Of course we can consider television, but with television you can speak here with no one present and then the tape will be put away on a shelf. Let's do it this way; you speak before our people and we'll speak before yours. This will be far better. They'll see and sense us. I'm setting a forum for you for the future.

Nixon: Yes. You must not be afraid of ideas.

Khrushchev: We keep telling you; don't you be afraid of ideas! We have nothing to fear. We've already escaped from that situation, and now we don't fear ideas.

Nixon: Well then let's have more exchange then. We all agree on that, right?

Khrushchev: Good. What do we agree to?

Nixon: Now let's go look at our pictures.

Khrushchev: I agree, but I want to make sure what I have agreed to. Do I have the right? I know that I'm dealing here with a very good lawyer. So, I want to hold up my coalminer's dignity so the coalminers would say: "That's our man, he doesn't yield to an American lawyer."

Nixon: No question about that.

Khrushchev: [Interrupts Nixon]: You are an advocate of capitalism, I am an advocate of communism! So let's compete!

Nixon: Yes. All that I can say is that from the way you talk and the way you dominate the conversation, you would have made a good lawyer yourself. But, what I mean is this: . . . the [recording] will transmit this very conversation immediately. And . . . this increase in communication will teach us some things, and will teach you some things too, because after all you do not know everything . . . .

Khrushchev: We are arguing on unequal ground. The camera is yours, you are speaking English and I am speaking Russian. Your English words are being taped and will be shown and heard, but what I am saying is being interpreted only in your ear, and therefore the American people won't hear what I've said. These are unequal conditions!

Nixon: There isn't a day that goes by in the United States when we can't read everything that you say in the Soviet Union . . . . I can assure you that you never make a statement here that you don't think we read in the United States.

Khrushchev: So then let it be so! I'll catch you on your words. Your words are taped. Translate my words, then we'll watch the tape with the English translation of what I've said to you in Russian . . . I would like that my words should also be translated into English. Do you give me your word?

Nixon: Now we have all of these reporters here. We have,

Khrushchev: [Interrupts Nixon]: No, do you give me your word?

Nixon: Every word that you have said has been taken down, and I will promise you that every word that you have said here will be reported in the United States and they will see you say it on television.

Khrushchev: But I have my doubts. Therefore, I want you, the Vice President, to give your word that my speech will also be recorded in English and broadcast. Will it?

Nixon: Certainly it will. Certainly.

[While inside the exhibit, Nixon and Khrushchev had the following exchange, as reported by the *New York Times*.]

Nixon [halting Khrushchev at model kitchen in model house]: "You had a very nice house in your exhibition in New York. My wife and I saw and enjoyed it very much. I want to show you this kitchen. It is like those of our houses in California."

Khrushchev [after Nixon called attention to a built-in panel-controlled washing machine]: "We have such things."

Nixon: "This is the newest model. This is the kind which is built in thousands of units for direct installation in the houses" . . . .

He explained that the house could be built for $14,000 and that most veterans had bought houses for between $10,000 and $15,000.

Nixon: "Let me give you an example . . . any steel worker could buy this house. They earn $3 an hour. This house costs about $100 a month to buy on a contract running twenty-five to thirty years.

Khrushchev: "We have steel workers and we have peasants who also can afford to spend $14,000 for a house." He said American houses were built to last only twenty years, so builders could sell new houses at the end of that period. "We build firmly. We build for our children and grandchildren."

Mr. Nixon said he thought American houses would last more than twenty years, but even so, after twenty years many Americans want a new home or a new kitchen, which would be obsolete then. The American system is designed to take advantage of new techniques, he said.

Document 19

Farewell Address
President Dwight D. Eisenhower
January 17, 1961

Dwight D. Eisenhower's Farewell Address is just as significant as his predecessor's (Document 14). Like Truman, Eisenhower devoted much of the speech to the Cold War, also placing the conflict into its historic context. He then turned to his primary thesis: a multi-faceted warning that the methods the nation chose to wage the Cold War should not undermine the very principles for which the United States stood and a way of life that valued individual liberty and initiative. Although Eisenhower can be criticized for overlooking his administration's own nurturing of the "military-industrial complex" he warned about through its nuclear weapons policy (Document 12), his speech had profound influence. Just one year later, for example, his warning was taken up and much modified by young activists who founded the Students for a Democratic Society (Document 22).

Source: Public Papers of the Presidents of the United States: Dwight D. Eisenhower, 1960-61 (Washington, D.C.: U.S. Government Printing Office, 1961), 1035-40. Available at https://goo.gl/VZ2UCg.

. . . This evening I come to you with a message of leave-taking and farewell, and to share a few final thoughts with you, my countrymen. . . .

We now stand ten years past the midpoint of a century that has witnessed four major wars among great nations. Three of these involved our own country. Despite these holocausts America is today the strongest, the most influential and most productive nation in the world. Understandably proud of this pre-eminence, we yet realize that America's leadership and prestige depend, not merely upon our unmatched material progress, riches and military strength, but on how we use our power in the interests of world peace and human betterment.

Throughout America's adventure in free government, our basic purposes have been to keep the peace; to foster progress in human achievement, and to enhance liberty, dignity and integrity among peoples and among nations. . . .

Progress toward these noble goals is persistently threatened by the conflict now engulfing the world. It commands our whole attention, absorbs our very beings. We face a hostile ideology – global in scope, atheistic in character, ruthless in purpose, and insidious in method. . . .

... [T]hreats, new in kind or degree, constantly arise. I mention two only.

A vital element in keeping the peace is our military establishment. Our arms must be mighty, ready for instant action, so that no potential aggressor may be tempted to risk his own destruction.

Our military organization today bears little relation to that known by any of my predecessors in peacetime, or indeed by the fighting men of World War II or Korea.

Until the latest of our world conflicts, the United States had no armaments industry. American makers of plowshares could, with time and as required, make swords as well. But now we can no longer risk emergency improvisation of national defense; we have been compelled to create a permanent armaments industry of vast proportions. Added to this, three and a half million men and women are directly engaged in the defense establishment. We annually spend on military security more than the net income of all United States corporations.

This conjunction of an immense military establishment and a large arms industry is new in the American experience. The total influence – economic, political, even spiritual – is felt in every city, every State house, every office of the Federal government. We recognize the imperative need for this development. Yet we must not fail to comprehend its grave implications. Our toil, resources and livelihood are all involved; so is the very structure of our society.

In the councils of government, we must guard against the acquisition of unwarranted influence, whether sought or unsought, by the military-industrial complex. The potential for the disastrous rise of misplaced power exists and will persist.

We must never let the weight of this combination endanger our liberties or democratic processes. We should take nothing for granted. Only an alert and knowledgeable citizenry can compel the proper meshing of the huge industrial and military machinery of defense with our peaceful methods and goals, so that security and liberty may prosper together.

Akin to, and largely responsible for the sweeping changes in our industrial-military posture, has been the technological revolution during recent decades.

In this revolution, research has become central; it also becomes more formalized, complex, and costly. A steadily increasing share is conducted for, by, or at the direction of, the Federal government.

Today, the solitary inventor, tinkering in his shop, has been overshadowed by task forces of scientists in laboratories and testing fields. In the same fashion, the free university, historically the fountainhead of free ideas and scientific discovery, has experienced a revolution in the conduct of research. Partly because of the huge costs involved, a government contract becomes virtually a substitute for intellectual curiosity. For every old blackboard there are now hundreds of new electronic computers.

The prospect of domination of the nation's scholars by Federal employment, project allocations, and the power of money is ever present – and is gravely to be regarded.

Yet, in holding scientific research and discovery in respect, as we should, we must also be alert to the equal and opposite danger that public policy could itself become the captive of a scientific-technological elite.

It is the task of statesmanship to mold, to balance, and to integrate these and other forces, new and old, within the principles of our democratic system – ever aiming toward the supreme goals of our free society. . . .

Document 20

Inaugural Address
President John F. Kennedy
January 20, 1961

The Cold War was a major influence on John F. Kennedy's Inaugural Address, shaping almost every paragraph. In a much-quoted passage, Kennedy referred to a new generation of Americans (himself included – he was just 44 years old upon taking the presidency) who would carry on the U.S. commitment to protecting liberty at home and expanding liberty abroad. Both of his predecessors, Presidents Truman and Eisenhower, had made and honored this commitment (Documents 2, 8, 14, 17, 19) but Kennedy suggested there was no limit to what the United States could – or would – do to advance its Cold War aims. At the same time, Kennedy called for a new spirit of international cooperation to aid in peaceful decolonization, global poverty reduction, and nuclear disarmament. Notable for its eloquence and brevity, the address also conveyed an optimism and confidence about the limitless power and ability of the United States to better the world at the start of a new decade. By the late 1960s, some of this optimism will have faded. For example, Kennedy authorized U.S. military action to help South Vietnam defend itself against a communist takeover (Document 21), but the difficulties and costs of that mission led President Nixon to offer a scaled-back statement of American global military commitments in 1969 (Document 34).

Source: John F. Kennedy, Inaugural Address, January 20, 1961. Available at https://goo.gl/tYv9zJ.

We observe today not a victory of party but a celebration of freedom – symbolizing an end as well as a beginning – signifying renewal as well as change. For I have sworn before you and Almighty God the same solemn oath our forbears prescribed nearly a century and three-quarters ago.

The world is very different now. For man holds in his mortal hands the power to abolish all forms of human poverty and all forms of human life. And yet the same revolutionary beliefs for which our forebears fought are still at issue around the globe – the belief that the rights of man come not from the generosity of the state but from the hand of God.

We dare not forget today that we are the heirs of that first revolution. Let the word go forth from this time and place, to friend and foe alike, that the torch has been passed to a new generation of Americans – born in this century, tempered by war, disciplined by a hard and bitter peace, proud of our ancient heritage – and unwilling to witness or permit the slow undoing of those human rights to which this nation has always been committed, and to which we are committed today at home and around the world.

Let every nation know, whether it wishes us well or ill, that we shall pay any price, bear any burden, meet any hardship, support any friend, oppose any foe to assure the survival and the success of liberty.

This much we pledge – and more.

To those old allies whose cultural and spiritual origins we share, we pledge the loyalty of faithful friends. United there is little we cannot do in a host of cooperative ventures. Divided there is little we can do – for we dare not meet a powerful challenge at odds and split asunder.

To those new states whom we welcome to the ranks of the free, we pledge our word that one form of colonial control shall not have passed away merely to be replaced by a far more iron tyranny. We shall not always expect to find them supporting our view. But we shall always hope to find them strongly supporting their own freedom – and to remember that, in the past, those who foolishly sought power by riding the back of the tiger ended up inside.

To those people in the huts and villages of half the globe struggling to break the bonds of mass misery, we pledge our best efforts to help them help themselves, for whatever period is required – not because the communists may be doing it, not because we seek their votes, but because it is right. If a free society cannot help the many who are poor, it cannot save the few who are rich.

To our sister republics south of our border, we offer a special pledge – to convert our good words into good deeds – in a new alliance for progress – to assist free men and free governments in casting off the chains of poverty. But this peaceful revolution of hope cannot become the prey of hostile powers. Let all our neighbors know that we shall join with them to oppose aggression or subversion anywhere in the Americas. And let every other power know that this Hemisphere intends to remain the master of its own house.

To that world assembly of sovereign states, the United Nations, our last best hope in an age where the instruments of war have far outpaced the instruments of peace, we renew our pledge of support – to prevent it from becoming merely a forum for invective – to strengthen its shield of the new and the weak – and to enlarge the area in which its writ may run.

Finally, to those nations who would make themselves our adversary, we offer not a pledge but a request: that both sides begin anew the quest for peace, before the dark powers of destruction unleashed by science engulf all humanity in planned or accidental self-destruction.

We dare not tempt them with weakness. For only when our arms are sufficient beyond doubt can we be certain beyond doubt that they will never be employed.

But neither can two great and powerful groups of nations take comfort from our present course – both sides overburdened by the cost of modern weapons, both rightly alarmed by the steady spread of the deadly atom, yet both racing to alter that uncertain balance of terror that stays the hand of mankind's final war.

So let us begin anew – remembering on both sides that civility is not a sign of weakness, and sincerity is always subject to proof. Let us never negotiate out of fear. But let us never fear to negotiate.

Let both sides explore what problems unite us instead of belaboring those problems which divide us.

Let both sides, for the first time, formulate serious and precise proposals for the inspection and control of arms – and bring the absolute power to destroy other nations under the absolute control of all nations.

Let both sides seek to invoke the wonders of science instead of its terrors. Together let us explore the stars, conquer the deserts, eradicate disease, tap the ocean depths and encourage the arts and commerce.

Let both sides unite to heed in all corners of the earth the command of Isaiah – to "undo the heavy burdens . . . (and) let the oppressed go free."

And if a beachhead of cooperation may push back the jungle of suspicion, let both sides join in creating a new endeavor, not a new balance of power, but a new world of law, where the strong are just and the weak secure and the peace preserved.

All this will not be finished in the first one hundred days. Nor will it be finished in the first one thousand days, nor in the life of this Administration, nor even perhaps in our lifetime on this planet. But let us begin.

In your hands, my fellow citizens, more than mine, will rest the final success or failure of our course. Since this country was founded, each generation of Americans has been summoned to give testimony to its national loyalty. The graves of young Americans who answered the call to service surround the globe.

Now the trumpet summons us again – not as a call to bear arms, though arms we need – not as a call to battle, though embattled we are – but a call to bear the burden of a long twilight struggle, year in and year out, "rejoicing in hope, patient in tribulation" – a struggle against the common enemies of man: tyranny, poverty, disease and war itself.

Can we forge against these enemies a grand and global alliance, North and South, East and West, that can assure a more fruitful life for all mankind? Will you join in that historic effort?

In the long history of the world, only a few generations have been granted the role of defending freedom in its hour of maximum danger. I do not shrink from this responsibility – I welcome it. I do not believe that any of us would exchange places with any other people or any other generation. The energy, the faith, the devotion which we bring to this endeavor will light our country and all who serve it – and the glow from that fire can truly light the world.

And so, my fellow Americans: ask not what your country can do for you – ask what you can do for your country.

My fellow citizens of the world: ask not what America will do for you, but what together we can do for the freedom of man.

Finally, whether you are citizens of America or citizens of the world, ask of us here the same high standards of strength and sacrifice which we ask of you. With a good conscience our only sure reward, with history the final judge of our deeds, let us go forth to lead the land we love, asking His blessing and His help, but knowing that here on earth God's work must truly be our own.

Document 21

Report to President Kennedy on South Vietnam
Dean Rusk and Robert McNamara
November 11, 1961

Like Korea, Vietnam was split in two, North and South, in the aftermath of World War II. France, aided by the United States, failed to reassert its colonial control after fighting insurgent forces in Vietnam led by Ho Chi Minh and supported by the Chinese. The Geneva Accords (1954), signed by the Democratic Republic of Vietnam (North Vietnam, a communist regime), France, the People's Republic of China, the Soviet Union, and the United Kingdom divided Vietnam at the 17th parallel and called for elections to be held by 1956 to reunite the country. Neither the United States nor the Republic of Vietnam (now in control of South Vietnam) accepted the Accords. The terms of the Accords were not honored by either side. The political and military struggle for control resumed.

By 1961, the United States had greatly increased its military and economic support of the government of Ngo Dinh Diem, the president of South Vietnam. Diem, though firmly anti-communist, had long struggled to secure the support of his people and establish the legitimacy of his regime. Government corruption and crackdowns on political opponents caused widespread unrest and deepened Diem's unpopularity. Meanwhile, the communist insurgency was growing in power in the South, as North Vietnam pressed its objective to unify Vietnam under its rule.

Authored by President Kennedy's Secretary of State, Dean Rusk, and Secretary of Defense, Robert McNamara, this report makes clear that U.S. policymakers believed the collapse of South Vietnam represented a grave threat to American and global security. Furthermore, should the United States fail to act, its credibility would suffer. Allies would question the commitment of the United States to protect them, and the fall of South Vietnam would lead to neighboring nations also becoming communist – the domino theory.

Rusk and McNamara recommended taking all necessary steps to contain the spread of communism to South Vietnam, including, if necessary, the deployment of U.S. combat forces to fight the growing communist insurgency. This proposal showed the militarization of containment at work (Documents 1 and 6). Rusk and McNamara hoped such a step could be avoided by providing more support for naval and ground force actions by the South Vietnamese military. By the date of this report, the United States had already stationed several thousand military advisers in Vietnam and 25 servicemen had died there. By late 1963, the number of advisers had

increased to 16,000 and 175 more Americans had been killed in the fighting. Despite
this support and more economic aid, the government of South Vietnam did not
stabilize nor did it defeat the communist insurgency.

Kennedy's assassination in November 1963 passed this problem on to President
Lyndon Johnson, who, in early 1965, made the fateful decision to send U.S. combat
forces to Vietnam (Documents 29–32). Yet the United States still struggled to stop
the communist revolution. As American casualties mounted, the war became
increasingly unpopular, adding to domestic tensions during the late 1960s
(Documents 33 and 34).

Source: The Pentagon Papers *as published by* The New York Times *(New*
York and Chicago: Quadrangle Books, 1971), 155–8. A photocopy of the original
"1961 Rusk-McNamara Report to Kennedy on South Vietnam" is available online
at the New York Times *Archive for July 1, 1971. https://goo.gl/2Zoxff.*

---

l. United States National Interests in South Viet-Nam.

The deteriorating situation in South Viet-Nam requires attention to the
nature and scope of United States national interests in that country. The loss of
South Viet-Nam to Communism would involve the transfer of a nation of 20
million people from the free world to the Communism bloc. The loss of South
Viet-Nam would make pointless any further discussion about the importance of
Southeast Asia to the free world; we would have to face the near certainty that
the remainder of Southeast Asia and Indonesia would move to a complete
accommodation with Communism, if not formal incorporation with the
Communist bloc. The United States, as a member of SEATO, has commitments
with respect to South Viet-Nam under the Protocol to the SEATO Treaty.[1]
Additionally, in a formal statement at the conclusion session of the 1954 Geneva
Conference, the United States representative stated that the United States
"would view any renewal of the aggression . . . with grave concern and seriously
threatening international peace and security."

The loss of South Viet-Nam to Communism would not only destroy
SEATO but would undermine the credibility of American commitments
elsewhere. Further, loss of South Viet-Nam would stimulate bitter domestic

---

[1] SEATO is the abbreviation for the Southeast Asia Treaty Organization. It was formed
in 1954. Its eight member states (United States, France, Great Britain, Philippines,
Thailand, Australia, New Zealand, and Pakistan) promised to stop the spread of
communism in Southeast Asia. The treaty establishing SEATO did not obligate
members to take military action; however, it did provide the United States with an
international justification for taking action in South Vietnam.

controversies in the United States and would be seized upon by extreme elements to divide the country and harass the Administration....

...

3. The United States' Objective in South Viet-Nam

The United States should commit itself to the clear objective of preventing the fall of South Viet-Nam to [communism]. The basic means for accomplishing this objective must be to put the Government of South Viet-Nam into a position to win its own war against the Guerrillas.[2] We must insist that that Government itself take the measures necessary for that purpose in exchange for large-scale United States assistance in the military, economic and political fields. At the same time we must recognize that it will probably not be possible for the GVN[3] to win this war as long as the flow of men and supplies from North Viet-Nam continues unchecked and the guerrillas enjoy a safe sanctuary in neighboring territory.

We should be prepared to introduce United States combat forces if that should become necessary for success. Dependent upon the circumstances, it may also be necessary for United States forces to strike at the source of the aggression in North Viet-Nam....

In the light of the foregoing, the Secretary of State and the Secretary of Defense recommend that:

1. We now take the decision to commit ourselves to the objective of preventing the fall of South Viet-Nam to Communism and that, in doing so, we recognize that the introduction of United States and other SEATO forces may be necessary to achieve this objective. (However, if it is necessary to commit outside forces to achieve the foregoing objective our decision to introduce United States forces should not be contingent upon unanimous SEATO agreement thereto.)

2. The Department of Defense be prepared with plans for the use of United States forces in South Viet Nam under one or more of the following purposes:

(a) Use of a significant number of United States forces to signify United States determination to defend Viet-Nam and to boost South Viet-Nam morale.

(b) Use of substantial United States forces to assist in suppressing Viet Cong insurgency short of engaging in detailed counter-guerrilla operations but including relevant operations in North Viet-Nam.

(c) Use of United States forces to deal with the situation if there is organized Communist military intervention....

---

[2] A reference to the Viet Cong, the communist insurgents in South Vietnam controlled by the North Vietnamese who used irregular, or guerilla, warfare strategies and tactics.

[3] Government of Vietnam, the term used to refer to the government in the South.

Document 22

The Port Huron Statement
Students for a Democratic Society
1962

In June 1962, a group of mostly white, middle-class college students met in Port Huron, Michigan, to draft a manifesto for the Students for a Democratic Society (SDS). SDS called for the creation of a "New Left," that is, a new kind of liberalism. As a Cold War document, the Port Huron Statement is significant for several reasons. First, it sharply challenged the nation's basic, bipartisan foreign policy: that every price must be paid, every effort made, to stop the global spread of communism. Second, the SDS became a vocal, well-organized opponent of the war in Vietnam (Documents 29–34). Third, by criticizing America's faith in technology, affluence, and materialism, the statement provided a foundation for the counterculture of the 1960s and beyond.

Source: Students for a Democratic Society, The Port Huron Statement *(New York: The Student Department of the League for Industrial Democracy, 1964).*

We are people of this generation, bred in at least modest comfort, housed now in universities, looking uncomfortably to the world we inherit.

When we were kids the United States was the wealthiest and strongest country in the world; the only one with the atom bomb, the least scarred by modern war, an initiator of the United Nations that we thought would distribute Western influence throughout the world. Freedom and equality for each individual, government of, by, and for the people – these American values we found good, principles by which we could live as men. Many of us began maturing in complacency.

As we grew, however, our comfort was penetrated by events too troubling to dismiss. First, the permeating and victimizing fact of human degradation, symbolized by the Southern struggle against racial bigotry, compelled most of us from silence to activism. Second, the enclosing fact of the Cold War, symbolized by the presence of the Bomb, brought awareness that we ourselves, and our friends, and millions of abstract "others" we knew more directly because of our common peril, might die at any time. We might deliberately ignore, or avoid, or fail to feel all other human problems, but not these two, for these were too immediate and crushing in their impact, too challenging in the demand that we as individuals take the responsibility for encounter and resolution.

While these and other problems either directly oppressed us or rankled our consciences and became our own subjective concerns, we began to see complicated and disturbing paradoxes in our surrounding America. The declaration "all men are created equal..." rang hollow before the facts of Negro life in the South and the big cities of the North. The proclaimed peaceful intentions of the United States contradicted its economic and military investments in the Cold War status quo....

Some would have us believe that Americans feel contentment amidst prosperity – but might it not better be called a glaze above deeply felt anxieties about their role in the new world? And if these anxieties produce a developed indifference to human affairs, do they not as well produce a yearning to believe there *is* an alternative to the present, that something *can* be done to change circumstances in the school, the workplaces, the bureaucracies, the government? It is to this latter yearning, at once the spark and engine of change, that we direct our present appeal. The search for truly democratic alternatives to the present, and a commitment to social experimentation with them, is a worthy and fulfilling human enterprise, one which moves us and, we hope, others today....

...As a *social system* we seek the establishment of a democracy of individual participation, governed by two central aims: that the individual share in those social decisions determining the quality and direction of his life; that society be organized to encourage independence in men and provide the media for their common participation.

In a participatory democracy, the political life would be based in several root principles:

> that decision-making of basic social consequence be carried on by public groupings;

> that politics be seen positively, as the art of collectively creating an acceptable pattern of social relations;

> that politics has the function of bringing people out of isolation and into community, thus being a necessary, though not sufficient, means of finding meaning in personal life; ...

The economic sphere would have as its basis the principles:

> that work should involve incentives worthier than money or survival....

that the economy itself is of such social importance that its major resources and means of production should be open to democratic participation and subject to democratic social regulation.

Like the political and economic ones, major social institutions – cultural, education, rehabilitative, and others – should be generally organized with the well-being and dignity of man as the essential measure of success.

In social change or interchange, we find violence to be abhorrent because it requires generally the transformation of the target, be it a human being or a community of people, into a depersonalized object of hate. It is imperative that the means of violence be abolished and the institutions – local, national, international – that encourage nonviolence as a condition of conflict be developed.

These are our central values, in skeletal form. It remains vital to understand their denial or attainment in the context of the modern world. . . .

Communism and Foreign Policy

As democrats we are in basic opposition to the communist system. The Soviet Union, as a system, rests on the total suppression organized opposition. . . . Communist parties throughout the rest of the world are generally undemocratic in internal structure and mode of action. . . .

But present trends in American anti-communism are not sufficient for the creation of appropriate policies with which to relate to and counter communist movements in the world. In no instance is this better illustrated than in our basic national policy-making assumption that the Soviet Union is inherently expansionist and aggressive, prepared to dominate the rest of the world by military means. On this assumption rests the monstrous American structure of military "preparedness"; because of it we sacrifice values and social programs to the alleged needs of military power. . . .

. . . [W]e can develop a fresh and creative approach to world problems which will help to create democracy at home and establish conditions for its growth elsewhere in the world.

Documents 23-26

The Cuban Missile Crisis
September-October, 1962

The Cuban Missile Crisis of October 1962 brought the world to the brink of nuclear war. These documents relate to the crisis's origins and tensest moments.

In the late 1950s, a revolution replaced Cuba's undemocratic government with a communist regime led by Fidel Castro. In the face of U.S. efforts to topple his regime, including support for a failed invasion by Cuban exiles at the Bay of Pigs (1961), Castro turned to the Soviet Union, which provided military assistance. The U.S. government closely monitored this aid, as seen in Document 23, dated September 4, 1962. In response to Castro's ties with the Soviets and support for revolution in Latin America, the Kennedy administration intensified covert operations against the Castro regime (Operation MONGOOSE), as seen in Document 24.

In September and October 1962, U.S. reconnaissance flights captured photographic evidence that the Soviet Union was secretly shipping nuclear warheads and missiles to Cuba and building launch bases there. President Kennedy convened a group of advisors (the Executive Committee of the National Security Council or ExComm) to provide recommendations on how to force the Soviet Union to remove the missiles, warheads, and bases. Document 25, dated October 19, considers the motives of the Soviet Union for the deployment and outlines several possible responses: an ultimatum to the Soviets to remove the bases, a naval blockade, or a surprise military attack.

Intense discussions within the ExComm produced a recommendation to blockade or quarantine the island nation of Cuba in order to prevent completion of the deployment. The ExComm and Kennedy also wanted to use the quarantine as leverage to force the removal of the missiles and warheads already in Cuba. Kennedy announced this action to the country in a televised address on October 22 (Document 26).

The Soviet Union only partially respected the quarantine. Tensions mounted; several generals openly advocated a military strike, not knowing that the Soviet commander in Cuba had the authority to use the nuclear weapons on the island to defend his forces. Had he used the weapons to retaliate against a U.S. military strike, a full nuclear war between the United States and the Soviet Union almost certainly would have broken out. However, Kennedy and Soviet Premier Nikita Khrushchev both continued to seek a peaceful end to the showdown. Letters between the two leaders opened the door to a resolution of the crisis. In exchange for an American *commitment to leave Castro alone, the Soviet Union would remove its nuclear weapons and bases. In a provision that was not made public, the United States also promised to remove nuclear missiles it had deployed at bases in Turkey, a U.S. ally. The crisis was over, but the danger of nuclear war in the future had not abated.*

Sources: Document 23: "United States Reaffirms Policy on Prevention of Aggressive Actions by Cuba," *Department of State Bulletin, Vol. 47, no. 1213 (September 24, 1962), 450. Available at https://goo.gl/1n7uRu.*

Document 24: *Laurence Chang and Peter Kornbluh, eds., "The Cuban Missile Crisis, 1962: The Documents" in* The Cuban Missile Crisis, 1962: The 40th Anniversary: A National Security Archive Documents Reader. *Available online at The National Security Archive, Washington, DC. https://goo.gl/kbezUC..*

Document 25: *Mary S. McAuliffe, ed., CIA Documents on the Cuban Missile Crisis 1962 (Washington, D.C.: History Staff, Central Intelligence Agency, 1992), 197-202. Available online from the Center for the Study of Intelligence. https://goo.gl/u91ER..*

Document 26: *"Radio and Television Report to the American People on the Soviet Arms Buildup in Cuba," October 22, 1962. Available online from Gerhard Peters and John T. Woolley, The American Presidency Project. https://goo.gl/mKfCVL.*

Document 23

Statement on Cuba
President John F. Kennedy
September 4, 1962

All Americans, as well as all of our friends in this hemisphere, have been concerned over the recent moves of the Soviet Union to bolster the military power of the Castro regime in Cuba. Information has reached this Government in the last 4 days from a variety of sources which establishes without doubt that the Soviets have provided the Cuban Government with a number of antiaircraft defense missiles with a slant range of 25 miles which are similar to early models of our Nike.[1] Along with these missiles, the Soviets are apparently providing the extensive radar and other electronic equipment which is required for their operation. We can also confirm the presence of several Soviet-made motor torpedo boats carrying ship-to-ship guided missiles having a range of 15 miles. The number of Soviet military technicians now known to be in Cuba or en route – approximately 3,500 – is consistent with assistance in setting up and learning to use this equipment. As I stated last week, we shall continue to make information available as fast as it is obtained and properly verified.

There is no evidence of any organized combat force in Cuba from any Soviet bloc country; of military bases provided to Russia; of a violation of the 1934 treaty relating to Guantanamo;[2] of the presence of offensive ground-to-ground missiles; or of other significant offensive capability either in Cuban hands or under Soviet direction and guidance. Were it to be otherwise, the gravest issues would arise.

The Cuban question must be considered as a part of the worldwide challenge posed by Communist threats to the peace. It must be dealt with as a part of that larger issue as well as in the context of the special relationships which have long characterized the inter-American system.

---

[1] Nike antiaircraft missiles, named after the Greek goddess of victory, were capable of downing Soviet long-range bombers carrying nuclear weapons. The United States built more than 200 Nike sites during the 1950s.

[2] A reference to the U.S. naval base at Guantanamo Bay, Cuba. The 1934 treaty allowed the United States to keep a base there as long as it wanted; Cuba could not cancel the lease without U.S. agreement.

It continues to be the policy of the United States that the Castro regime will not be allowed to export its aggressive purposes by force or the threat of force. It will be prevented by whatever means may be necessary from taking action against any part of the Western Hemisphere. The United States, in conjunction with other hemisphere countries, will make sure that while increased Cuban armaments will be a heavy burden to the unhappy people of Cuba themselves, they will be nothing more.

Document 24

Minutes of the Meeting of the Special Group (Augmented) on Operation MONGOOSE

October 4, 1962

4 October 1962

MEMORANDUM FOR RECORD

SUBJECT: Minutes of Meeting of the Special Group (Augmented) on Operation MONGOOSE, 4 October 1962

PRESENT: The Attorney General; Mr. Johnson; Mr. Gilpatric, General Taylor, General Lansdale; Mr. McCone and General Carter . . .[1]

1. The Attorney General opened the meeting by saying that higher authority <u>is concerned about progress on the MONGOOSE program and feels that more priority should be given to trying to mount sabotage operations.</u>[2] The Attorney General said that he wondered if a new look is not required at this time in view of the meager results, especially in the sabotage field. He urged that "massive activity" be mounted within the entire MONGOOSE framework. There was a good deal of discussion about this, and General Lansdale said that another attempt will be made against the major target which has been the object of three unsuccessful missions, and that approximately six new ones are in the planning stage.

   Mr. Johnson said that "massive activity" would have to appear to come from within. He also said that he hopes soon to be able to present to the Group a plan

---

[1] The president's brother Robert F. Kennedy was the Attorney General. U. Alexis Johnson was Deputy Under Secretary of State for Political Affairs; Roswell L. Gilpatric was Deputy Secretary of Defense; General Maxwell D. Taylor was the President's Military Representative; Brigadier General Edward G. Lansdale was Chief of Operations for Operation MONGOOSE; John A. McCone was Director of the CIA; and Lt. General Marshall S. Carter was Deputy Director of the CIA.

[2] Underlining in original

for giving Cuban exiles more of a free hand, with the full realization that this would give more visibility to their activities. . . .

2. Mr. McCone then said that he gets the impression that high levels of the government want to get on with activity but still wish to retain a low noise level. He does not believe that this will be possible. Any sabotage would be blamed on the United States. . . . He urged that responsible officials be prepared to accept a higher noise level if they want to get on with operations. . . .

3. Returning to Mr. Johnson's point about the necessity of massive activity coming from within, Mr. McCone pointed out that internal security missions are now so rigid that internal uprisings are sure to be brutally suppressed. It was agreed that the current guidelines do not call for inciting such an uprising.

4. Mr. McCone and General Carter explained the tremendous efforts which are necessary to insure that an operation such as the sabotage one previously authorized cannot be pinned directly on the U.S. After considerable discussion, the Group agreed that it is not necessary to go to such extreme lengths to guarantee non-attributability and that short cuts will be acceptable.

5. Mr. Gilpatric reported that Defense is now working hard on establishing a Cuban brigade. Recruits will be trained for four or five months and will then be on call for any future action.

6. General Taylor reported that the Joint Staff is refining various military contingency plans, based on a variety of possible situations. Such situations include: Soviet action against Berlin; presence of Bloc offensive weapons in Cuba; attack against Guantanamo; a popular uprising; armed Cuban subversion in the Hemisphere; and the establishment of a direct threat to the U.S.

7. The Group then turned to the subject of reconnaissance of Cuba. . . . It was pointed out that the Agency [CIA] is now restricted to using its high performance vehicle in the southeast quadrant of Cuba, because of the SAM sites.[3] It was questioned whether this is a reasonable restriction at this time, particularly when the SAMs are almost certainly not operational. . . .

8. There was some discussion of the desirability of mining Cuban waters. It was pointed out that non-U.S.-attributable mines, which appear to be homemade, are available and could be laid by small craft operated by Cubans.

---

[3] Surface-to-air missiles, used to destroy aircraft.

9. It was agreed that the Attorney General should act as Chairman of the Special Group (Augmented) at least <u>for the time being</u>.
10. It was agreed that four major points emerged from today's discussion:
    a. We ought to go all out for increased intelligence.
    b. There should be <u>considerably more sabotage.</u>
    c. Restrictions on attributability can be relaxed so that training and other preparations can be subject to some short cuts.
    d. <u>All efforts should be made to develop new and imaginative approaches to the possibility of getting rid of the Castro regime.</u>

Document 25

Soviet Reactions to Certain U.S. Courses of Action on Cuba

Central Intelligence Agency
October 19, 1962

The Problem

To estimate probable Soviet reactions to certain US courses of action with respect to Cuba.

The Estimate

1. A major Soviet objective in their military buildup in Cuba is to demonstrate that the world balance of forces has shifted so far in their favor that the US can no longer prevent the advance of Soviet offensive power even into its own hemisphere. In this connection they assume, of course, that these deployments sooner or later will become publicly known.

2. It is possible that the USSR is installing these missiles primarily in order to use them in bargaining for US concessions elsewhere. We think this unlikely, however. The public withdrawal of Soviet missiles from Cuba would create serious problems in the USSR's relations with Castro; it would cast doubt on the firmness of the Soviet intention to protect the Castro regime and perhaps on their commitments elsewhere.

3. If the US accepts the strategic missile buildup in Cuba, the Soviets would continue the buildup of strategic weapons in Cuba. We have no basis for estimating the force level which they would wish to reach, but it seems clear already that they intend to go beyond a token capability. . . .

4. US acceptance of the strategic missile buildup would provide strong encouragement to Communists, pro-Communists, and the more anti-American sectors of opinion in Latin America and elsewhere. Conversely, anti-Communists and those who relate their own interests to those of the US would be strongly discouraged. It seems clear that, especially over the long run, there would be a loss of confidence in US power and determination and a serious decline of US influence generally.

Effect of Warning

5. If the US confronts Khrushchev with its knowledge of the MRBM[1] deployment and presses for a withdrawal, we do not believe the Soviets would halt the deployment. Instead, they would propose negotiations on the general question of foreign bases, claiming equal right to establish Soviet bases and assuring the US of tight control over the missiles. . . .

6. There is some slight chance that a warning to Castro might make a difference, since the Soviets could regard this as a chance to stand aside, but it also would give time for offers to negotiate, continued buildup, and counter pressures, and we think the result in the end would be the same.

7. Any warning would of course degrade the element of surprise in a subsequent US attack.

Effect of Blockade

8. While the effectiveness of Castro's military machine might be impaired by a total US blockade, Castro would be certain to tighten internal security and would take ruthless action against any attempts at revolt. There is no reason to believe that a blockade of itself would bring down the Castro regime. The Soviets would almost certainly exert strong direct pressures elsewhere to end the blockade. . . .

Soviet Reaction to Use of Military Force

9. If the US takes direct military action against Cuba, the Soviets would be placed automatically under great pressure to respond in ways which, if they could not save Cuba, would inflict an offsetting injury to US interests. This would be true whether the action was limited to an effort to neutralize the strategic missiles, or these missiles plus airfields, surface-to-air missile sites, or cruise missile sites, or in fact an outright invasion designed to destroy the Castro regime.

10. In reaction to any of the various forms of US action, the Soviets would be alarmed and agitated, since they have to date estimated that the US would not take military action in the face of Soviet warnings of the danger of nuclear war. They would recognize that US military action posed a major challenge to the prestige of the USSR. We must of course recognize the possibility that the Soviets, under pressure to respond, would again miscalculate and respond in a way which, through a series of actions and reactions, could escalate to general war.

11. On the other hand, the Soviets have no public treaty with Cuba and have not acknowledged that Soviet bases are on the island. This situation provides

---

[1] Medium-Range Ballistic Missiles, which had a maximum range of approximately 1,100 miles.

them with a pretext for treating US military action against Cuba as an affair which does not directly involve them, and thereby avoiding the risks of a strong response. We do not believe that the USSR would attack the US, either from Soviet bases or with its missiles in Cuba, even if the latter were operational and not put out of action before they could be readied for firing.

12. Since the USSR would not dare to resort to general war and could not hope to prevail locally, the Soviets would almost certainly consider retaliatory actions outside Cuba. The timing and selection of such moves would depend heavily upon the immediate context of events and the USSR's appreciation of US attitudes....

13. We believe that whatever course of retaliation the USSR elected, the Soviet leaders would not deliberately initiate general war or take military measures, which in their calculation, would run the gravest risks of general war.

Document 26

Radio and Television Report to the American People on the Soviet Arms Buildup in Cuba

President John F. Kennedy
October 22, 1962

Good evening, my fellow citizens:

This Government, as promised, has maintained the closest surveillance of the Soviet military buildup on the island of Cuba. Within the past week, unmistakable evidence has established the fact that a series of offensive missile sites is now in preparation on that imprisoned island. The purpose of these bases can be none other than to provide a nuclear strike capability against the Western Hemisphere. . . .

The characteristics of these new missile sites indicate two distinct types of installations. Several of them include medium range ballistic missiles, capable of carrying a nuclear warhead for a distance of more than 1,000 nautical miles.[1] Each of these missiles, in short, is capable of striking Washington, D. C., the Panama Canal, Cape Canaveral, Mexico City, or any other city in the southeastern part of the United States, in Central America, or in the Caribbean area. . . .

This urgent transformation of Cuba into an important strategic base – by the presence of these large, long-range, and clearly offensive weapons of sudden mass destruction – constitutes an explicit threat to the peace and security of all the Americas . . . . This action also contradicts the repeated assurances of Soviet spokesmen, both publicly and privately delivered, that the arms buildup in Cuba would retain its original defensive character, and that the Soviet Union had no need or desire to station strategic missiles on the territory of any other nation.
. . .

Neither the United States of America nor the world community of nations can tolerate deliberate deception and offensive threats on the part of any nation, large or small. We no longer live in a world where only the actual firing of weapons represents a sufficient challenge to a nation's security to constitute maximum peril. Nuclear weapons are so destructive and ballistic missiles are so

---

[1] A nautical mile is about 15 percent longer than a regular mile.

swift, that any substantially increased possibility of their use or any sudden change in their deployment may well be regarded as a definite threat to peace.

. . .

The 1930's taught us a clear lesson: aggressive conduct, if allowed to go unchecked, ultimately leads to war. This nation is opposed to war. We are also true to our word. Our unswerving objective, therefore, must be to prevent the use of these missiles against this or any other country, and to secure their withdrawal or elimination from the Western Hemisphere.

Our policy has been one of patience and restraint, as befits a peaceful and powerful nation, which leads a worldwide alliance. We have been determined not to be diverted from our central concerns by mere irritants and fanatics. But now further action is required – and it is under way; and these actions may only be the beginning. We will not prematurely or unnecessarily risk the costs of worldwide nuclear war in which even the fruits of victory would be ashes in our mouth – but neither will we shrink from that risk at any time it must be faced.

Acting, therefore, in the defense of our own security and of the entire Western Hemisphere, and under the authority entrusted to me by the Constitution as endorsed by the resolution of the Congress, I have directed that the following initial steps be taken immediately:

First: To halt this offensive buildup, a strict quarantine on all offensive military equipment under shipment to Cuba is being initiated. All ships of any kind bound for Cuba from whatever nation or port will, if found to contain cargoes of offensive weapons, be turned back. This quarantine will be extended, if needed, to other types of cargo and carriers. We are not at this time, however, denying the necessities of life as the Soviets attempted to do in their Berlin blockade of 1948.

Second: I have directed the continued and increased close surveillance of Cuba and its military buildup. The foreign ministers of the OAS,[2] in their communiqué of October 6, rejected secrecy on such matters in this hemisphere. Should these offensive military preparations continue, thus increasing the threat to the hemisphere, further action will be justified. I have directed the Armed Forces to prepare for any eventualities; and I trust that in the interest of both the Cuban people and the Soviet technicians at the sites, the hazards to all concerned of continuing this threat will be recognized.

Third: It shall be the policy of this Nation to regard any nuclear missile launched from Cuba against any nation in the Western Hemisphere as

---

[2] The Organization of American States (OAS), founded in 1948, included almost all the nations of the Western Hemisphere. One of the purposes of the OAS is to help resolve conflict between member states.

an attack by the Soviet Union on the United States, requiring a full retaliatory response upon the Soviet Union. . . .

. . . I call upon Chairman Khrushchev[3] to halt and eliminate this clandestine, reckless, and provocative threat to world peace and to stable relations between our two nations. I call upon him further to abandon this course of world domination, and to join in an historic effort to end the perilous arms race and to transform the history of man. He has an opportunity now to move the world back from the abyss of destruction – by returning to his government's own words that it had no need to station missiles outside its own territory, and withdrawing these weapons from Cuba – by refraining from any action which will widen or deepen the present crisis – and then by participating in a search for peaceful and permanent solutions. . . .

Finally, I want to say a few words to the captive people of Cuba, to whom this speech is being directly carried by special radio facilities. I speak to you as a friend, as one who knows of your deep attachment to your fatherland, as one who shares your aspirations for liberty and justice for all. And I have watched and the American people have watched with deep sorrow how your nationalist revolution was betrayed – and how your fatherland fell under foreign domination. Now your leaders are no longer Cuban leaders inspired by Cuban ideals. They are puppets and agents of an international conspiracy which has turned Cuba against your friends and neighbors in the Americas . . . .

. . . I have no doubt that most Cubans today look forward to the time when they will be truly free – free from foreign domination, free to choose their own leaders, free to select their own system, free to own their own land, free to speak and write and worship without fear or degradation. And then shall Cuba be welcomed back to the society of free nations and to the associations of this hemisphere.

My fellow citizens: let no one doubt that this is a difficult and dangerous effort on which we have set out. No one can foresee precisely what course it will take or what costs or casualties will be incurred. Many months of sacrifice and self-discipline lie ahead – months in which both our patience and our will will be tested – months in which many threats and denunciations will keep us aware of our dangers. But the greatest danger of all would be to do nothing. . . .

---

[3] Nikita Khrushchev, the leader of the Soviet Union.

Document 27

Remarks in the Rudolph Wilde Platz, Berlin
President John F. Kennedy
June 26, 1963

At the end of World War II, the United States, Great Britain, the Soviet Union, and France divided defeated Germany into four zones; each Allied power governed one of these zones. This division was duplicated in the German capital of Berlin. In 1949, the American, British, and French zones unified to become one nation, the Federal Republic of Germany, more commonly called West Germany. The Soviet zone became the German Democratic Republic or East Germany. West Germany was a democratic, capitalist state, allied with the United States; East Germany, an ally of the Soviet Union, was communist. Berlin, no longer the capital, also was divided into two parts, East and West. West Berlin was the sovereign territory of West Germany, but it was located inside East Germany. From 1949 to 1961, West Berlin served as an escape route for East Germans who did not want to live under communism. In 1961, the Soviets ordered the East German government to build a wall around West Berlin to prevent any more escapes.

President Kennedy's visit to West Berlin in June 1963 served several purposes. First, it demonstrated continuing American support for the residents of West Berlin. Second, it offered an opportunity to criticize communism. If communism was such an ideal system, why were so many fleeing it? Third, the speech allowed the United States to reiterate its basic Cold War aim, to advance the cause of freedom, an aim reiterated in 1987 by Ronald Reagan (Document 43).

Source: Public Papers of the Presidents: John F. Kennedy, 1963 *(Washington, D.C.: U.S. Government Printing Office, 1964), 524-5.*

I am proud to come to this city as the guest of your distinguished Mayor, who has symbolized throughout the world the fighting spirit of West Berlin. And I am proud to visit the Federal Republic with your distinguished Chancellor who for so many years has committed Germany to democracy and freedom and progress . . . . Today, in the world of freedom, the proudest boast is "Ich bin ein Berliner" [I am a Berliner].

I appreciate my interpreter translating my German!

There are many people in the world who really don't understand, or say they don't, what is the great issue between the free world and the Communist world. Let them come to Berlin. There are some who say that communism is the wave of the future. Let them come to Berlin. And there are some who say in Europe and elsewhere we can work with the Communists. Let them come to Berlin. And there are even a few who say that it is true that communism is an evil system, but it permits us to make economic progress. . . . Let them come to Berlin.

Freedom has many difficulties and democracy is not perfect, but we have never had to put a wall up to keep our people in, to prevent them from leaving us. I want to say, on behalf of my countrymen, who live many miles away on the other side of the Atlantic, who are far distant from you, that they take the greatest pride that they have been able to share with you, even from a distance, the story of the last 18 years. I know of no town, no city, that has been besieged for 18 years that still lives with the vitality and the force, and the hope and the determination of the city of West Berlin. While the wall is the most obvious and vivid demonstration of the failures of the Communist system, for all the world to see, we take no satisfaction in it, for it is, as your Mayor has said, an offense not only against history but an offense against humanity, separating families, dividing husbands and wives and brothers and sisters, and dividing a people who wish to be joined together.

What is true of this city is true of Germany – real, lasting peace in Europe can never be assured as long as one German out of four is denied the elementary right of free men, and that is to make a free choice. In 18 years of peace and good faith, this generation of Germans has earned the right to be free, including the right to unite their families and their nation in lasting peace, with good will to all people. You live in a defended island of freedom, but your life is part of the main. So let me ask you, as I close, to lift your eyes beyond the dangers of today, to the hopes of tomorrow, beyond the freedom merely of this city of Berlin, or your country of Germany, to the advance of freedom everywhere, beyond the wall to the day of peace with justice, beyond yourselves and ourselves to all mankind.

Freedom is indivisible, and when one man is enslaved, all are not free. When all are free, then we can look forward to that day when this city will be joined as one and this country and this great Continent of Europe in a peaceful and hopeful globe. When that day finally comes, as it will, the people of West Berlin can take sober satisfaction in the fact that they were in the front lines for almost two decades.

All free men, wherever they may live, are citizens of Berlin, and, therefore, as a free man, I take pride in the words "Ich bin ein Berliner!"

Document 28

Limited Test Ban Treaty
August 5, 1963

The 1962 Cuban Missile Crisis (Documents 23–26) vividly exposed the hazards of nuclear weapons. Although neither the United States nor the Soviet Union tried to negotiate a disarmament treaty after the crisis, the two powers, along with Great Britain, did draft and sign an agreement to limit the testing of new nuclear weapons. The treaty allowed tests but prohibited a signatory from carrying out nuclear explosions that would send fallout beyond its borders or territory. It also banned underwater, atmospheric, and space detonations. The treaty had no expiration and it was open to other nations. By the end of 1963, more than 120 other nations had signed the treaty.

Source: United States Treaties and Other International Agreements, *Vol. 14, part 2 (Washington, D.C.: U.S. Government Printing Office, 1964), 1313–19.*

Treaty Banning Nuclear Weapon Tests in the Atmosphere, in Outer Space and Under Water

The Governments of the United States of America, the United Kingdom of Great Britain and Northern Ireland, and the Union of Soviet Socialist Republics, hereinafter referred to as the "Original Parties,"

Proclaiming as their principal aim the speediest possible achievement of an agreement on general and complete disarmament under strict international control in accordance with the objectives of the United Nations which would put an end to the armaments race and eliminate the incentive to the production and testing of all kinds of weapons, including nuclear weapons,

Seeking to achieve the discontinuance of all test explosions of nuclear weapons for all time, determined to continue negotiations to this end, and desiring to put an end to the contamination of man's environment by radioactive substances,

Have agreed as follows:

Article I

1. Each of the Parties to this Treaty undertakes to prohibit, to prevent, and not to carry out any nuclear weapon test explosion, or any other nuclear explosion, at any place under its jurisdiction or control:

(a) in the atmosphere; beyond its limits, including outer space; or underwater, including territorial waters or high seas; or

(b) in any other environment if such explosion causes radioactive debris to be present outside the territorial limits of the State under whose jurisdiction or control such explosion is conducted. . . .

2. Each of the Parties to this Treaty undertakes furthermore to refrain from causing, encouraging, or in any way participating in, the carrying out of any nuclear weapon test explosion, or any other nuclear explosion, anywhere which would take place in any of the environments described, or have the effect referred to, in paragraph 1 of this Article.

Article II

1. Any Party may propose amendments to this Treaty. . . .

2. Any amendment to this Treaty must be approved by a majority of the votes of all the Parties to this Treaty, including the votes of all of the Original Parties. . . .

Article III

1. This Treaty shall be open to all States for signature. Any State which does not sign this Treaty before its entry into force in accordance with paragraph 3 of this Article may accede to it at any time.

2. This Treaty shall be subject to ratification by signatory States. . . .

Article IV

This Treaty shall be of unlimited duration.

Each Party shall in exercising its national sovereignty have the right to withdraw from the Treaty if it decides that extraordinary events, related to the subject matter of this Treaty, have jeopardized the supreme interests of its country. It shall give notice of such withdrawal to all other Parties to the Treaty three months in advance. . . .

Documents 29-30

Gulf of Tonkin Incident
August 5-7, 1964

During 1964, the U.S. military provided concealed support for South Vietnamese commando actions against North Vietnamese military targets. Known as Operations Plan 34A, the raids had two basic purposes: one, to block North Vietnam's support of the communist insurgency in South Vietnam; and two, to demonstrate the United States' willingness to use military force on behalf of its ally (Document 21). The raids were not effective. They did provoke a response, however. On August 2, 1964, North Vietnamese gunboats fired on the U.S. destroyer Maddox, which was monitoring North Vietnamese communications in the Gulf of Tonkin, off the coast of North Vietnam. Aware of American support for the commando raids, North Vietnam targeted the Maddox to show its readiness to strike back at U.S. forces. The Maddox defended itself, sinking two North Vietnamese gunboats. Two days later, another U.S. destroyer, the Turner Joy, reported being attacked, but that incident was not confirmed; the Turner Joy's electronic equipment may have misinterpreted weather disturbances as a torpedo attack.

President Lyndon Johnson ordered retaliatory air attacks against North Vietnamese targets and delivered an address to Congress on August 5, 1964 (Document 29). Johnson described the attack on U.S. warships, but in a significant and intentional omission, he did not say anything about Operation Plan 34A, thus giving the impression that North Vietnam's strike was unprovoked. Johnson asked Congress for a joint resolution authorizing the president, as commander-in-chief, to use all necessary measures, including military force, to prevent further communist aggression in Southeast Asia. Two days later, on August 7, Congress complied. All members of the House who were present and all but two senators voted to approve the Gulf of Tonkin Resolution (Document 30). The resolution negated the need to declare war in Vietnam and opened the door to send large numbers of U.S. troops to Vietnam.

Sources: Public Papers of the Presidents of the United States: Lyndon B. Johnson, 1963-64, *Book II (Washington, D.C.: U.S. Government Printing Office, 1965), 930-2. Available at https://goo.gl/eLEmv3.*

Department of State Bulletin, Vol. 51, no. 1313 (August 24, 1964), 268.

Document 29

Special Message to the Congress on U.S. Policy in Southeast Asia

President Lyndon B. Johnson

August 5, 1964

To the Congress of the United States:

Last night I announced to the American people that the North Vietnamese regime had conducted further deliberate attacks against U.S. naval vessels operating in international waters, and that I had therefore directed air action against gun boats and supporting facilities used in these hostile operations.[1] This air action has now been carried out with substantial damage to the boats and facilities. Two U.S. aircraft were lost in the action.

After consultation with the leaders of both parties in the Congress, I further announced a decision to ask the Congress for a Resolution expressing the unity and determination of the United States in supporting freedom and in protecting peace in Southeast Asia.

These latest actions of the North Vietnamese regime have given a new and grave turn to the already serious situation in Southeast Asia. Our commitments in that area are well known to the Congress. They were first made in 1954 by President Eisenhower. They were further defined in the Southeast Asia Collective Defense Treaty approved by the Senate in February 1955.[2]

This treaty with its accompanying protocol obligates the United States and other members to act in accordance with their Constitutional processes to meet Communist aggression against any of the parties or protocol states.

Our policy in southeast Asia has been consistent and unchanged since 1954. I summarized it on June 2 in four simple propositions:

1. *America keeps her word.* Here as elsewhere, we must and shall honor our commitments.

2. *The issue is the future of Southeast Asia as a whole.* A threat to any nation in that region is a threat to all, and a threat to us.

---

[1] The president here refers to the North Vietnamese attack on the *USS Maddox*; see the introductory note to the document.

[2] For an explanation of this treaty, see the first footnote for Document 21.

3. *Our purpose is peace.* We have no military, political or territorial ambitions in the area.

4. *This is not just a jungle war, but a struggle for freedom on every front of human activity.* Our military and economic assistance to South Vietnam and Laos in particular has the purpose of helping these countries to repel aggression and strengthen their independence.

The threat to the three nations of southeast Asia has long been clear. The North Vietnamese regime has constantly sought to take over South Vietnam and Laos. This Communist regime has violated the Geneva Accords for Vietnam. It has systematically conducted a campaign of subversion, which includes the direction, training, and supply of personnel and arms for the conduct of guerrilla warfare in South Vietnamese territory. In Laos, the North Vietnamese regime has maintained military forces, used Laotian territory for infiltration into South Vietnam, and most recently carried out combat operations – all in direct violation of the Geneva Agreements of 1962.[3]

In recent months, the actions of the North Vietnamese regime have become steadily more threatening. . . .

As President of the United States I have concluded that I should now ask the Congress, on its part, to join in affirming the national determination that all such attacks will be met, and that the U.S. will continue in its basic policy of assisting the free nations of the area to defend their freedom.

As I have repeatedly made clear, the United States intends no rashness, and seeks no wider war. We must make it clear to all that the United States is united in its determination to bring about the end of Communist subversion and aggression in the area. We seek the full and effective restoration of the international agreements signed in Geneva in 1954, with respect to South Vietnam, and again in Geneva in 1962, with respect to Laos.

I recommend a Resolution expressing the support of the Congress for all necessary action to protect our armed forces and to assist nations covered by the SEATO Treaty. At the same time, I assure the Congress that we shall continue readily to explore any avenues of political solution that will effectively guarantee the removal of Communist subversion and the preservation of the independence of the nations of the area.

The Resolution could . . . state in the simplest terms the resolve and support of the Congress for action to deal appropriately with attacks against our armed

---

[3] In May 1954, the Vietnamese communists decisively defeated French forces at Dien Bien Phu in northern Vietnam. Under an agreement known as the Geneva Accords, France agreed to begin a phased withdrawal from its colony, which was divided in half at the 17th parallel. The Viet Minh governed Vietnam north of this line; a noncommunist regime had power in the south. See the introduction to Document 21.

forces and to defend freedom and preserve peace in Southeast Asia in accordance with the obligations of the United States under the Southeast Asia Treaty. I urge the Congress to enact such a resolution promptly and thus to give convincing evidence to the aggressive Communist nations, and to the world as a whole, that our policy in Southeast Asia will be carried forward – and that the peace and security of the area will be preserved.

The events of this week would in any event have made the passage of a Congressional Resolution essential. But there is an additional reason for doing so at a time when we are entering on three months of political campaigning. Hostile nations must understand that in such a period the United States will continue to protect its national interests, and that in these matters there is no division among us.

Document 30

Joint Resolution of Congress, H.J. RES 1145
August 7, 1964

. . . Resolved by the Senate and House of Representatives of the United States of America in Congress assembled,

That the Congress approves and supports the determination of the President, as Commander in Chief, to take all necessary measures to repel any armed attack against the forces of the United States and to prevent further aggression.

Section 2. The United States regards as vital to its national interest and to world peace the maintenance of international peace and security in southeast Asia. Consonant with the Constitution of the United States and the Charter of the United Nations and in accordance with its obligations under the Southeast Asia Collective Defense Treaty, the United States is, therefore, prepared, as the President determines, to take all necessary steps, including the use of armed force, to assist any member or protocol state of the Southeast Asia Collective Defense Treaty requesting assistance in defense of its freedom.

Section 3. This resolution shall expire when the President shall determine that the peace and security of the area is reasonably assured by international conditions created by action of the United Nations or otherwise, except that it may be terminated earlier by concurrent resolution of the Congress.

Document 31

"Peace Without Conquest"
President Lyndon B. Johnson
April 7, 1965

In early 1965, as the government of South Vietnam appeared to be losing to insurgent forces supported by North Vietnam, President Johnson made the decision to send U.S. combat forces to Vietnam and to bomb North Vietnamese targets using U.S. aircraft and crews. In April 1965, Johnson gave this televised address at Johns Hopkins University in Baltimore, Maryland, to explain why the United States was fighting in Vietnam. Like his predecessors, Johnson presented the conflict in Vietnam as a major test of American determination to stop the spread of aggression. He compared the war to the actions taken by the United States to protect Europe during and after World War II.

Source: Address at Johns Hopkins University: "Peace Without Conquest," April 7, 1965, Public Papers of the Presidents of the United States: Lyndon B. Johnson, 1965, Book I (Washington, D.C. : U. S. Government Printing Office, 1966), 394–399. Available online from Gerhard Peters and John T. Woolley, The American Presidency Project. https://goo.gl/p9vRYJ.

. . . Tonight Americans and Asians are dying for a world where each people may choose its own path to change.

This is the principle for which our ancestors fought in the valleys of Pennsylvania.[1] It is the principle for which our sons fight tonight in the jungles of Viet-Nam.

Viet-Nam is far away from this quiet campus. We have no territory there, nor do we seek any. The war is dirty and brutal and difficult. And some 400 young men, born into an America that is bursting with opportunity and promise, have ended their lives on Viet-Nam's steaming soil.

Why must we take this painful road?

Why must this Nation hazard its ease, and its interest, and its power for the sake of a people so far away?

---

[1] A reference to the American Revolution.

We fight because we must fight if we are to live in a world where every country can shape its own destiny. And only in such a world will our own freedom be finally secure.

This kind of world will never be built by bombs or bullets. Yet the infirmities of man are such that force must often precede reason, and the waste of war, the works of peace.

We wish that this were not so. But we must deal with the world as it is, if it is ever to be as we wish.

The Nature of the Conflict

The world as it is in Asia is not a serene or peaceful place.

The first reality is that North Viet-Nam has attacked the independent nation of South Viet-Nam. Its object is total conquest.

Of course, some of the people of South Viet-Nam are participating in attack on their own government. But trained men and supplies, orders and arms, flow in a constant stream from north to south.

This support is the heartbeat of the war.

And it is a war of unparalleled brutality. Simple farmers are the targets of assassination and kidnapping. Women and children are strangled in the night because their men are loyal to their government. . . .

Over this war – and all Asia – is another reality: the deepening shadow of Communist China. The rulers in Hanoi are urged on by Peking.[2] This is a regime which has destroyed freedom in Tibet, which has attacked India, and has been condemned by the United Nations for aggression in Korea. It is a nation which is helping the forces of violence in almost every continent. The contest in Viet-Nam is part of a wider pattern of aggressive purposes.

Why Are We in Viet-Nam?

Why are these realities our concern? Why are we in South Viet-Nam?

We are there because we have a promise to keep. Since 1954 every American President has offered support to the people of South Viet-Nam. We have helped to build, and we have helped to defend. Thus, over many years, we have made a national pledge to help South Viet-Nam defend its independence.

And I intend to keep that promise.

To dishonor that pledge, to abandon this small and brave nation to its enemies, and to the terror that must follow, would be an unforgivable wrong.

We are also there to strengthen world order. Around the globe, from Berlin to Thailand, are people whose well-being rests, in part, on the belief that they

---

[2] A reference to communist China, officially called the People's Republic of China.

can count on us if they are attacked. To leave Viet-Nam to its fate would shake the confidence of all these people in the value of an American commitment and in the value of America's word. The result would be increased unrest and instability, and even wider war.

We are also there because there are great stakes in the balance. Let no one think for a moment that retreat from Viet-Nam would bring an end to conflict. The battle would be renewed in one country and then another. The central lesson of our time is that the appetite of aggression is never satisfied. To withdraw from one battlefield means only to prepare for the next. We must say in southeast Asia – as we did in Europe – in the words of the Bible: "Hitherto shalt thou come, but no further."[3] ...

Our Objective in Viet-Nam

Our objective is the independence of South Viet-Nam, and its freedom from attack. We want nothing for ourselves – only that the people of South Viet-Nam be allowed to guide their own country in their own way.

We will do everything necessary to reach that objective. And we will do only what is absolutely necessary....

We hope that peace will come swiftly. But that is in the hands of others besides ourselves. And we must be prepared for a long continued conflict. It will require patience as well as bravery, the will to endure as well as the will to resist. ...

The Dream of World Order

This will be a disorderly planet for a long time. In Asia, as elsewhere, the forces of the modern world are shaking old ways and uprooting ancient civilizations. There will be turbulence and struggle and even violence. Great social change – as we see in our own country now – does not always come without conflict....

Conclusion

... Every night before I turn out the lights to sleep I ask myself this question: Have I done everything that I can do to unite this country? Have I done everything I can to help unite the world, to try to bring peace and hope to all the peoples of the world? Have I done enough?

Ask yourselves that question in your homes – and in this hall tonight. Have we, each of us, all done all we could? Have we done enough? ...

---

[3] A reference to the Old Testament of the Bible: Job 38:11.

This generation of the world must choose: destroy or build, kill or aid, hate or understand.

We can do all these things on a scale never dreamed of before.

Well, we will choose life.[4] In so doing we will prevail over the enemies within man, and over the natural enemies of all mankind. . . .

---

[4] Deuteronomy 30:19

Document 32

A Compromise Solution For South Vietnam
George Ball
July 1, 1965

George Ball was an undersecretary of state for agricultural and economic affairs, who had previously been a strong supporter of U.S aid to South Vietnam. By 1965, Ball had come to doubt the ability of the United States to prevent the unification of Vietnam under communism. In this memorandum to President Johnson's National Security Adviser, McGeorge Bundy, Ball explained his doubts. Ball's warning that the United States would not prevail in Vietnam proved prophetic. The problems he foresaw helped drive Johnson from the presidency. It would fall to his successor, President Richard Nixon, to find a way out of the war (Document 37).

Source: Document 40, The Foreign Relations of the United States, 1964-1968, Vol. III, Vietnam, June-December 1965, *(Washington, D.C.: U.S. Department of State, Office of the Historian, 1996), 107-13. Available at https://goo.gl/K94wPZ.*

A Losing War: The South Vietnamese are losing the war to the Viet Cong.[1] No one can assure you that we can beat the Viet Cong or even force them to the conference table on our terms no matter how many hundred thousand white foreign (US) troops we deploy.

No one has demonstrated that a white ground force of whatever size can win a guerrilla war – which is at the same time a civil war between Asians – in jungle terrain in the midst of a population that refuses cooperation to the white forces (and the SVN)[2] and thus provides a great intelligence advantage to the other side. . . .

The Question to Decide: Should we limit our liabilities in South Viet-Nam and try to find a way out with minimal long-term costs?

The alternative – no matter what we may wish it to be – is almost certainly a protracted war involving an open-ended commitment of US forces, mounting US casualties, no assurance of a satisfactory solution, and a serious danger of escalation at the end of the road.

---

[1] Viet Cong was a common name used to refer to the South Vietnamese communists.

[2] SVN was an abbreviation for the government of South Vietnam, the United States' ally.

Need for a Decision Now: So long as our forces are restricted to advising and assisting the South Vietnamese, the struggle will remain a civil war between Asian peoples. Once we deploy substantial numbers of troops in combat it will become a war between the United States and a large part of the population of South Viet-Nam, organized and directed from North Viet-Nam and backed by the resources of both Moscow and Peiping.

The decision you [McGeorge Bundy, the National Security Adviser] face now, therefore, is crucial. Once large numbers of US troops are committed to direct combat they will begin to take heavy casualties in a war they are ill-equipped to fight in a non-cooperative if not downright hostile countryside.

Once we suffer large casualties we will have started a well-nigh irreversible process. Our involvement will be so great that we cannot – without national humiliation – stop short of achieving our complete objectives. Of the two possibilities I think humiliation would be more likely than the achievement of our objectives – even after we had paid terrible costs.

A Compromise Solution: Should we commit US manpower and prestige to a terrain so unfavorable as to give a very large advantage to the enemy – or should we seek a compromise settlement which achieves less than our stated objectives and thus cut our losses while we still have the freedom of maneuver to do so?

Costs of Compromise Solution: The answer involves a judgment as to the costs to the United States of such a compromise settlement in terms of our relations with the countries in the area of South Viet-Nam, the credibility of our commitments and our prestige around the world. In my judgment, if we act before we commit substantial US forces to combat in South Viet-Nam we can, by accepting some short-term costs, avoid what may well be a long-term catastrophe. I believe we have tended greatly to exaggerate the costs involved in a compromise settlement. . . .

Document 33

Statement by the Student Nonviolent Coordinating Committee on the War in Vietnam
January 6, 1966

A group of college students founded the Student Nonviolent Coordinating Committee (SNCC) in April 1960 to capitalize on the peaceful sit-ins they had just led to end segregation in restaurants in Nashville, Tennessee. Within a few years, SNCC had organized numerous civil rights campaigns, including the 1961 Freedom Rides, which successfully pressured the Kennedy administration to enforce a Supreme Court decision banning the racial segregation of interstate travel, and the 1964 Freedom Summer voter registration drive. In early 1965, SNCC joined with the Reverend Martin Luther King, Jr., and the Southern Christian Leadership Conference to register black voters in Selma, Alabama. The hazards faced by SNCC were often deadly. In Mississippi, for example, Klansmen murdered three SNCC members for registering black voters.

The murder of African American civil rights activist Samuel Younge, Jr., on January 3, 1966, led SNCC to issue the following position paper. As a Cold War document, the statement links the escalating war in Vietnam (Documents 29–32) to the ongoing Civil Rights Movement. SNCC raises sharp questions about the purposes of the war in Vietnam. Was the United States really fighting for the freedom of the Vietnamese people? How could the nation profess to be a force of liberty in the world when it had not yet guaranteed freedom and equality for African Americans?

Source: Wisconsin Historical Society, Freedom Summer Collection, Lucile Montgomery Papers, 1963-1967, Historical Society Library Microforms Room, Micro 44, Reel 3, Segment 48. Available at https://goo.gl/mUw2Nr.

The Student Nonviolent Coordinating Committee has a right and a responsibility to dissent with United States foreign policy on any issue when it sees fit. The Student Nonviolent Coordinating Committee now states its opposition to the United States' involvement in Vietnam on these grounds:

We believe the United States government has been deceptive in its claims of concern for the freedom of the Vietnamese people, just as the government has been deceptive in claiming concern for the freedom of colored people in such other countries as the Dominican Republic, the Congo, South Africa, Rhodesia[1], and in the United States itself.

We, the Student Nonviolent Coordinating Committee, have been involved in the black peoples' struggle for liberation and self-determination in this country for the past five years. Our work, particularly in the South, has taught us that the United States government has never guaranteed the freedom of oppressed citizens, and is not yet truly determined to end the rule of terror and oppression within its own borders.

We ourselves have often been victims of violence and confinement executed by United States governmental officials. We recall the numerous persons who have been murdered in the South because of their efforts to secure their civil and human rights, and whose murderers have been allowed to escape penalty for their crimes.

The murder of Samuel Young in Tuskegee, Alabama, is no different than the murder of peasants in Vietnam, for both Young and the Vietnamese sought, and are seeking, to secure the rights guaranteed them by law.[2] In each case, the United States government bears a great part of the responsibility for these deaths.

Samuel Young was murdered because United States law is not being enforced. Vietnamese are murdered because the United States is pursuing an aggressive policy in violation of international law. The United States is no respecter of persons or law when such persons or laws run counter to its needs or desires.

We recall the indifference, suspicion and outright hostility with which our reports of violence have been met in the past by government officials.

We know that for the most part, elections in this country, in the North as well as the South, are not free. We have seen that [*recent civil rights laws*] have not yet been implemented with full federal power and sincerity.

We question, then, the ability and even the desire of the United States government to guarantee free elections abroad. We maintain that our country's cry of "preserve freedom in the world" is a hypocritical mask, behind which it squashes liberation movements which are not bound, and refuse to be bound, by the expediencies of United States cold war policies.

---

[1] Now known as Zimbabwe.

[2] Samuel Younge, Jr., (his name was misspelled in the original), age 21, was shot and killed in Macon County, Alabama, by a gas station attendant for trying to use a white-only restroom. A Navy veteran, Younge was a student at the Tuskegee Institute and was active in civil rights campaigns, including a voter registration drive. His murder led to mass protests and the release of SNCC's position paper. Younge's killer was indicted in November 1966 but was acquitted by an all-white jury.

We are in sympathy with, and support, the men in this country who are unwilling to respond to a military draft which would compel them to contribute their lives to United States aggression in Vietnam in the name of the "freedom" we find so false in this country.

We recoil with horror at the inconsistency of a supposedly "free" society where responsibility to freedom is equated with the responsibility to lend oneself to military aggression. We take note of the fact that 16 percent of the draftees from this country are Negroes called on to stifle the liberation of Vietnam, to preserve a "democracy" which does not exist for them at home.

We ask, where is the draft for the freedom fight in the United States?

We therefore encourage those Americans who prefer to use their energy in building democratic forms within this country. We believe that work in the civil rights movement and with other human relations organizations is a valid alternative to the draft. We urge all Americans to seek this alternative, knowing full well that it may cost them their lives – as painfully as in Vietnam.

Document 34

Address to the Nation on the War in Vietnam

President Richard M. Nixon

November 3, 1969

As a candidate for the presidency in 1968, Richard Nixon campaigned in part on a promise to end the war in Vietnam. This speech, delivered eleven months after his inauguration, provided the details of his plan to withdraw the United States from the conflict. Although the military situation had improved for U.S. and South Vietnamese forces, domestic support for the war continued to erode. Echoing his predecessor Lyndon Johnson, Nixon spoke of the need to demonstrate American determination to keep its promises; otherwise, instability and violence would spread globally. He also announced a new policy: Vietnamization or the Nixon Doctrine. According to this policy, the United States would assist in the defense of other nations, but those nations would have to supply the manpower for their defense. The Nixon Doctrine was thus a return to something like the Truman Doctrine (Document 2). It showed a recognition that, contrary to the assumptions of earlier Cold War policies such as NSC 68 (Document 6), and the rhetoric of Kennedy's Inaugural Address (Document 20), the United States did not have unlimited resources to fight the Cold War. Acknowledging the effect of the anti-war demonstrations and seeking a counterweight, Nixon finished his speech by evoking "the great silent majority of" Americans who, he hoped, would support his efforts to end the war on terms acceptable to the United States. In a swipe at war opponents, the president also remarked, "North Vietnam cannot defeat or humiliate the United States. Only Americans can do that."

Source: Public Papers of the Presidents of the United States: Richard Nixon, 1969 *(Washington, D.C.: U.S. Government Printing Office, 1971), 901–9. Available online at Richard Nixon Presidential Library and Museum.* https://goo.gl/WwSY6R.

Good evening, my fellow Americans:

Tonight I want to talk to you on a subject of deep concern to all Americans and to many people in all parts of the world – the war in Vietnam.

. . .

. . . I would like to answer some of the questions that I know are on the minds of many of you listening to me.

How and why did America get involved in Vietnam in the first place?

How has this administration changed the policy of the previous administration?

What has really happened in the negotiations in Paris[1] and on the battlefront in Vietnam?

What choices do we have if we are to end the war?

What are the prospects for peace?

Now, let me begin by describing the situation I found when I was inaugurated on January 20.

– The war had been going on for 4 years.

– 31,000 Americans had been killed in action.

– The training program for the South Vietnamese was behind schedule.

– 540,000 Americans were in Vietnam with no plans to reduce the number.

– No progress had been made at the negotiations in Paris and the United States had not put forth a comprehensive peace proposal.

– The war was causing deep division at home and criticism from many of our friends as well as our enemies abroad.

In view of these circumstances there were some who urged that I end the war at once by ordering the immediate withdrawal of all American forces.

From a political standpoint this would have been a popular and easy course to follow. . . .

. . . [but] I had to think of the effect of my decision on the next generation and on the future of peace and freedom in America and in the world.

Let us all understand that the question before us is not whether some Americans are for peace and some are against peace. The question at issue is not whether Johnson's war becomes Nixon's war.

The great question is: How can we win America's peace?

Well, let us turn now to the fundamental issue. Why and how did the United States become involved in Vietnam in the first place?

Fifteen years ago North Vietnam, with the logistical support of Communist China and the Soviet Union, launched a campaign to impose a Communist government on South Vietnam by instigating and supporting a revolution.

In response to the request of the Government of South Vietnam, President Eisenhower sent economic aid and military equipment to assist the people of South Vietnam in their efforts to prevent a Communist takeover. Seven years ago, President Kennedy sent 16,000 military personnel to Vietnam as combat

---

[1] Representatives of the United States and North Vietnam began meeting in Paris in 1968 to negotiate an end to the war, but little progress had been made by the time of President Nixon's speech.

advisers. Four years ago, President Johnson sent American combat forces to South Vietnam. . . .

. . . Now that we are in the war, what is the best way to end it?

In January I could only conclude that the precipitate withdrawal of American forces from Vietnam would be a disaster not only for South Vietnam but for the United States and the cause of peace.

For the South Vietnamese, our precipitate withdrawal would inevitably allow the Communists to repeat the massacres which followed their takeover in the North 15 years before . . .

For the United States, this first defeat in our Nation's history would result in a collapse of confidence in American leadership, not only in Asia but throughout the world. . . .

For these reasons, I rejected the recommendation that I should end the war by immediately withdrawing all of our forces. I chose instead to change American policy on both the negotiating front and battlefront.

In order to end a war fought on many fronts, I initiated a pursuit for peace on many fronts.

In a television speech on May 14, in a speech before the United Nations, and on a number of other occasions I set forth our peace proposals in great detail.

– We have offered the complete withdrawal of all outside forces within 1 year.

– We have proposed a cease-fire within 1 year.

– We have offered free elections under international supervision with the Communists participating in the organization and conduct of the elections as an organized political force. And the Saigon Government[2] has pledged to accept the result of the elections. . . .

Hanoi[3] has refused even to discuss our proposals. They demand our unconditional acceptance of their terms, which are that we withdraw all American forces immediately and unconditionally and that we overthrow the Government of South Vietnam as we leave. . . .

Well now, who is at fault?

It has become clear that the obstacle in negotiating an end to the war is not the President of the United States. It is not the South Vietnamese Government.

The obstacle is the other side's absolute refusal to show the least willingness to join us in seeking a just peace. And it will not do so while it is convinced that all it has to do is to wait for our next concession, and our next concession after that one, until it gets everything it wants. . . .

---

[2] The government of South Vietnam.
[3] The government of North Vietnam. Hanoi was its capital.

Now let me turn, however, to a more encouraging report on another front.

At the time we launched our search for peace I recognized we might not succeed in bringing an end to the war through negotiation. I, therefore, put into effect another plan to bring peace – a plan which will bring the war to an end regardless of what happens on the negotiating front.

It is in line with a major shift in U.S. foreign policy which I described in my press conference at Guam on July 25. Let me briefly explain what has been described as the Nixon Doctrine – a policy which not only will help end the war in Vietnam, but which is an essential element of our program to prevent future Vietnams. . . .

. . . – First, the United States will keep all of its treaty commitments.

– Second, we shall provide a shield if a nuclear power threatens the freedom of a nation allied with us or of a nation whose survival we consider vital to our security.

– Third, in cases involving other types of aggression, we shall furnish military and economic assistance when requested in accordance with our treaty commitments. But we shall look to the nation directly threatened to assume the primary responsibility of providing the manpower for its defense.

. . .

The defense of freedom is everybody's business – not just America's business. And it is particularly the responsibility of the people whose freedom is threatened. In the previous administration, we Americanized the war in Vietnam. In this administration, we are Vietnamizing the search for peace.

. . . [T]he primary mission of our troops is [now] to enable the South Vietnamese forces to assume the full responsibility for the security of South Vietnam. . . .

. . . As South Vietnamese forces become stronger, the rate of American withdrawal can become greater. . . .

My fellow Americans, I am sure you can recognize from what I have said that we really only have two choices open to us if we want to end this war.

– I can order an immediate, precipitate withdrawal of all Americans from Vietnam without regard to the effects of that action.

– Or we can persist in our search for a just peace through a negotiated settlement if possible, or through continued implementation of our plan for Vietnamization if necessary – a plan in which we will withdraw all of our forces from Vietnam on a schedule in accordance with our program, as the South Vietnamese become strong enough to defend their own freedom.

I have chosen the second course.

It is not the easy way.

It is the right way . . .

And now I would like to address a word, if I may, to the young people of this Nation who are particularly concerned, and I understand why they are concerned, about this war.

I respect your idealism.

I share your concern for peace.

I want peace as much as you do . . .

I have chosen a plan for peace. I believe it will succeed.

If it does succeed, what the critics say now won't matter. If it does not succeed, anything I say then won't matter.

I know it may not be fashionable to speak of patriotism or national destiny these days. But I feel it is appropriate to do so on this occasion.

Two hundred years ago this Nation was weak and poor. But even then, America was the hope of millions in the world. Today we have become the strongest and richest nation in the world. And the wheel of destiny has turned so that any hope the world has for the survival of peace and freedom will be determined by whether the American people have the moral stamina and the courage to meet the challenge of free world leadership. . . .

And so tonight – to you, the great silent majority of my fellow Americans – I ask for your support. . . .

Let us be united for peace. Let us also be united against defeat. Because let us understand: North Vietnam cannot defeat or humiliate the United States. Only Americans can do that. . . .

Document 35

Telephone Conversation about Chile
Henry Kissinger and William Rogers
September 14, 1970

After the communist revolution in Cuba in 1959 (Documents 23–24), U.S. leaders were determined to prevent the rise of additional communist regimes in Latin America. This goal was consistent with the long-standing policy of containment (Documents 1–2), but it complicated inter-American relations. The United States, for example, pressured other nations in the Western Hemisphere, including Chile, to break all ties with Cuba.

Chile was a constitutional democracy. It also had active communist and socialist parties (though the communist party was banned from 1948 – 1957). Foreign corporations owned 25 percent of Chile's industry and dominated the most important sector of the economy, copper mining. In September 1970, in a three-way race, Salvador Allende won a plurality of votes for president. This meant that the Chilean Congress had to decide among the candidates, which by custom meant choosing the one who had received the most votes. Allende assumed office in November 1970. Allende promised to implement a political and economic program he called the "Chilean Road to Socialism" that included more state control of the economy and nationalization of the copper industry. Though a drastic economic change, this program was implemented through Chile's established governing framework; Allende relied on a left-wing coalition government to pass the necessary laws.

Allende was not a communist, but his actions greatly alarmed the Nixon administration, as seen in this conversation between Nixon's National Security Adviser, Henry Kissinger, and his Secretary of State, William Rogers. Speaking just after it appeared that Allende had won Chile's election, the officials made it clear that they wanted to prevent Allende from taking office and that they were willing to use covert operations to achieve this goal (Document 16). This was not the only time during the Cold War that the United States took action against a regime it saw as a threat (Document 24). For the outcome of the U.S. actions taken in response to Allende's election, see the introductory note for Document 38.

Source: National Security Archive, Electronic Briefing Book no. 255 (September 10, 2008). Available at https://goo.gl/Bfwimb.

[Rogers]: Okay. On Chile, CIA has prepared a paper with general conclusions which I think are pretty good – our people agree. But whatever we do, I think there are two things we should take into consideration: one, we want to be sure the paper record doesn't look bad. No matter what we do it will probably end up dismal. So our paper work should be done carefully. [Next sentence blacked out in original.] I talked with the President [Nixon] at length about it. My feeling – and I think it coincides with the President's – is that we ought to encourage a different result from the _____ [blank in original] but should do so discreetly so that it doesn't backfire.

[Kissinger]: The only question is how one defines "backfire."

[Rogers]: Getting caught doing something. After all we've said about elections, if the first time a Communist wins the U.S. tries to prevent the constitutional process from coming into play we will look very bad.

[Kissinger]: The President's view is to do the maximum possible to prevent an Aliente [Allende] takeover, but through Chilean sources and with a low posture.

[Rogers]: I have been disturbed by Corry's [Korry's] telegrams. They sound frenetic and somewhat irrational. I know that he's under pressure but we ought to be careful of him. He's got tender nerve ends. I don't know if you saw his telegrams.[1]

[Kissinger]: Yes, I did.

[Rogers]: And I think we've got to be sure he acts with discretion. He's a high-strung fellow.

[Kissinger]: I think what we have to do is make a cold-blooded assessment, get a course of action this week some time and then get it done.

[Rogers]: I talked to [name removed in original]. I think it's important that he understand that what he's doing is not his doing but encouraging the Chileans to do what they should. If it's our project as distinguished from Chilean it's going to be bad from us. I'm not sure he's the best man to do it. I'm not sure he's the most discreet fellow. [Next sentence blacked out in original.]

[Kissinger]: Is it?

[Rogers]: Not that I know of right now. We ought, as you say, to cold-bloodedly decide what to do and then do it.

---

[1] Edward M. Korry was the U.S. ambassador to Chile from 1967 – 1971.

Document 36

Joint Statement Following Discussions with Leaders of the People's Republic of China (Shanghai Communiqué)

February 27, 1972

During his presidency, Richard Nixon reshaped the U.S. Cold War position into a policy known as détente (a French word that means an easing of tensions). Détente was not an abandonment of containment – the United States still remained committed to halting the spread of communism – but the policy did mean the United States would identify international problems that it could resolve through diplomatic negotiation with communist rivals, especially the Soviet Union and China. Nixon also hoped that détente would make the Soviet Union and China less likely to aggressively advance global communism. Prime examples of détente included a nuclear arms reduction agreement with the Soviet Union (the Strategic Arms Limitation Treaty of 1972), a deal to sell surplus U.S. wheat to the Soviet Union, and, as seen in the document below, a move to normalize relations between the United States and the People's Republic of China.

Nixon's 1972 meeting with China's communist leader Mao Tse-Tung, which was secretly arranged, was bold and surprising. The United States had severed diplomatic ties with China after Mao came to power. Both nations had fought one another during the Korean War (Documents 8–9), and the United States remained an ally of Taiwan, which China wanted to annex. (Taiwan, a democracy, was populated by ethnic Chinese.) The United States had two primary purposes in reaching out to communist China: to create trade opportunities for U.S. goods in China (a goal that dated to the late nineteenth century) and to coax China into pressuring its ally North Vietnam to accept the terms of the United States to end the Vietnam War (Document 34).

Nixon's trip did result in increased cultural contact and helped set up the restoration of diplomatic ties in 1979. It served as the foundation for current relations between the United States and China, which include close economic ties (though not as envisioned: the U.S. now has a trade deficit with China) and consultation on the continuing issue of a divided Korea. The trip did not, however, help the United States obtain the terms it wanted to end the war in Vietnam (Document 37). Détente also proved short-lived. Nixon's resignation in 1974 as a result of the Watergate scandal took away the policy's leading advocate, while the Soviet invasion of Afghanistan in late 1979 renewed American concerns that the Soviets were again seeking global domination through the aggressive spread of communism (Document 41).

Source: Document 203, The Foreign Relations of the United States, 1969 – 1972, Vol. XVII, China, 1969-1972 (*Washington, D.C.: U.S. Department of State, Office of the Historian, 2006), 812-16. Available at https://goo.gl/PnydHT.*

President Richard Nixon of the United States of America visited the People's Republic of China at the invitation of Premier Chou Enlai of the People's Republic of China from February 21 to February 28, 1972. Accompanying the President were Mrs. Nixon, U.S. Secretary of State William Rogers, Assistant to the President Dr. Henry Kissinger, and other American officials.

President Nixon met with Chairman Mao Tse-tung of the Communist Party of China on February 21. The two leaders had a serious and frank exchange of views on Sino-U.S. relations and world affairs.

During the visit, extensive, earnest, and frank discussions were held between President Nixon and Premier Chou En-lai on the normalization of relations between the United States of America and the People's Republic of China, as well as on other matters of interest to both sides. In addition, Secretary of State William Rogers and Foreign Minister Chi P'eng-fei held talks in the same spirit.

President Nixon and his party visited Peking and viewed cultural, industrial and agricultural sites, and they also toured Hangchow and Shanghai where, continuing discussions with Chinese leaders, they viewed similar places of interest.

The leaders of the People's Republic of China and the United States of America found it beneficial to have this opportunity, after so many years without contact, to present candidly to one another their views on a variety of issues. They reviewed the international situation in which important changes and great upheavals are taking place and expounded their respective positions and attitudes.

The U.S. side stated: Peace in Asia and peace in the world requires efforts both to reduce immediate tensions and to eliminate the basic causes of conflict. The United States will work for a just and secure peace: just, because it fulfills the aspirations of peoples and nations for freedom and progress; secure, because it removes the danger of foreign aggression. The United States supports individual freedom and social progress for all the peoples of the world, free of outside pressure or intervention. The United States believes that the effort to reduce tensions is served by improving communication between countries that have different ideologies so as to lessen the risks of confrontation through accident, miscalculation or misunderstanding. Countries should treat each other with mutual respect and be willing to compete peacefully, letting performance be the ultimate judge. No country should claim infallibility and each country should be prepared to re-examine its own attitudes for the common good. The United States stressed that the peoples of Indochina should be allowed to determine their destiny without outside intervention . . . . The United States will maintain its close ties with and support for the Republic of Korea; the United States will support efforts of the Republic of Korea to seek a relaxation of tension and increased communication in the Korean peninsula. The United States places the highest value on its friendly relations with Japan; it will continue to develop the existing close bonds. . . .

The Chinese side stated: Wherever there is oppression, there is resistance. Countries want independence, nations want liberation and the people want revolution – this has become the irresistible trend of history. All nations, big or small, should be equal; big nations should not bully the small and strong nations should not bully the weak. China will never be a superpower and it opposes hegemony and power politics of any kind. The Chinese side stated that it firmly supports the struggles of all the oppressed people and nations for freedom and liberation and that the people of all countries have the right to choose their social systems according to their own wishes and the right to safeguard the independence, sovereignty and territorial integrity of their own countries and oppose foreign aggression, interference, control and subversion. All foreign troops should be withdrawn to their own countries.

The Chinese side expressed its firm support to the peoples of Vietnam, Laos, and Cambodia in their efforts for the attainment of their goal . . . . It firmly opposes the revival and outward expansion of Japanese militarism and firmly supports the Japanese people's desire to build an independent, democratic, peaceful and neutral Japan. . . .

There are essential differences between China and the United States in their social systems and foreign policies. However, the two sides agreed that countries, regardless of their social systems, should conduct their relations on the principles of respect for the sovereignty and territorial integrity of all states, nonaggression against other states, noninterference in the internal affairs of other states, equality and mutual benefit, and peaceful coexistence. International disputes should be settled on this basis, without resorting to the use or threat of force. The United States and the People's Republic of China are prepared to apply these principles to their mutual relations.

With these principles of international relations in mind the two sides stated that:

– progress toward the normalization of relations between China and the United States is in the interests of all countries;

– both wish to reduce the danger of international military conflict;

– neither should seek hegemony in the Asia–Pacific region and each is opposed to efforts by any other country or group of countries to establish such hegemony; and

– neither is prepared to negotiate on behalf of any third party or to enter into agreements or understandings with the other directed at other states.

Both sides are of the view that it would be against the interests of the peoples of the world for any major country to collude with another against other countries, or for major countries to divide up the world into spheres of interest.

The two sides reviewed the long-standing serious disputes between China and the United States. The Chinese side reaffirmed its position: The Taiwan question is the crucial question obstructing the normalization of relations between China and the United States; the Government of the People's Republic of China is the sole legal government of China; Taiwan is a province of China which has long been returned to the motherland; the liberation of Taiwan is China's internal affair in which no other country has the right to interfere; and all U.S. forces and military installations must be withdrawn from Taiwan. The Chinese Government firmly opposes any activities which aim at the creation of "one China, one Taiwan," "one China, two governments," "two Chinas," and "independent Taiwan" or advocate that "the status of Taiwan remains to be determined."

The U.S. side declared: The United States acknowledges that all Chinese on either side of the Taiwan Strait maintain there is but one China and that Taiwan is a part of China. The United States Government does not challenge that position. It reaffirms its interest in a peaceful settlement of the Taiwan question by the Chinese themselves. With this prospect in mind, it affirms the ultimate objective of the withdrawal of all U.S. forces and military installations from Taiwan. In the meantime, it will progressively reduce its forces and military installations on Taiwan as the tension in the area diminishes. . . .

Both sides view bilateral trade as another area from which mutual benefit can be derived, and agreed that economic relations based on equality and mutual benefit are in the interest of the people of the two countries. They agree to facilitate the progressive development of trade between their two countries.

. . .

Document 37

Address to the Nation Announcing Conclusion of an Agreement on Ending the War and Restoring Peace in Vietnam

President Richard M. Nixon

January 23, 1973

Throughout its first term, the Nixon administration struggled to end the war in Vietnam. By 1972, most U.S. troops had been withdrawn, as Nixon had promised (Document 34), but the bombing of North Vietnam continued in an effort to force its leaders to accept a peace treaty recognizing the independence of South Vietnam. By late 1972, an agreement was finally at hand; both sides accepted it in January 1973. Nixon described the agreement as "peace with honor," but Vietnam remained in a state of war. Congress refused to fund continued assistance (economic aid and military weapons) to South Vietnam, which was unable to halt the advance of communist forces. Hampered by the growing Watergate scandal, Nixon was not able to order bombing in support of the South Vietnamese government. In April 1975, the United States evacuated its embassy in Saigon, South Vietnam, as North Vietnamese troops captured the city. The South Vietnamese government fell, and Vietnam was unified under communist rule, fulfilling the goal the Vietnamese communists had had since 1945.

The costs of the war – billions of dollars, domestic turmoil, and more than 58,000 U.S. military deaths – continued to shape U.S. Cold War policies and politics for years to come. For instance, while President Ronald Reagan later defended the war as a worthy fight, President Jimmy Carter called it an example of the "intellectual and moral poverty" of automatically resorting to military force to achieve Cold War aims (Document 40).

Source: Public Papers of the Presidents of the United States: Richard Nixon, 1973 (Washington, D.C.: U.S. Government Printing Office, 1975), 18–20. Available online from Gerhard Peters and John T. Woolley, The American Presidency Project. https://goo.gl/qnvNLV.

I have asked for this radio and television time tonight for the purpose of announcing that we today have concluded an agreement to end the war and bring peace with honor in Vietnam and in Southeast Asia.

The following statement is being issued at this moment in Washington and Hanoi:

At 12:30 Paris time today, January 23, 1973, the Agreement on Ending the War and Restoring Peace in Vietnam was initialed by Dr. Henry Kissinger on behalf of the United States, and Special Adviser Le Duc Tho on behalf of the Democratic Republic of Vietnam [*North Vietnam*]....

... [T]he United States and the Democratic Republic of Vietnam [*South Vietnam*] express the hope that this agreement will insure stable peace in Vietnam and contribute to the preservation of lasting peace in Indochina and Southeast Asia.

That concludes the formal statement. Throughout the years of negotiations, we have insisted on peace with honor. In my addresses to the Nation from this room of January 25 and May 8 [1972], I set forth the goals that we considered essential for peace with honor.

In the settlement that has now been agreed to, all the conditions that I laid down then have been met.

A cease-fire, internationally supervised, will begin at 7 p.m., this Saturday, January 27, Washington time.

Within 60 days from this Saturday, all Americans held prisoners of war throughout Indochina will be released. There will be the fullest possible accounting for all of those who are missing in action.

During the same 60-day period, all American forces will be withdrawn from South Vietnam.

The people of South Vietnam have been guaranteed the right to determine their own future, without outside interference....

We shall continue to aid South Vietnam within the terms of the agreement and we shall support efforts by the people of South Vietnam to settle their problems peacefully among themselves.

We must recognize that ending the war is only the first step toward building the peace. All parties must now see to it that this is a peace that lasts, and also a peace that heals – and a peace that not only ends the war in Southeast Asia but contributes to the prospects of peace in the whole world.

This will mean that the terms of the agreement must be scrupulously adhered to. We shall do everything the agreement requires of us and we shall expect the other parties to do everything it requires of them. We shall also expect other interested nations to help insure that the agreement is carried out and peace is maintained.

As this long and very difficult war ends, I would like to address a few special words to each of those who have been parties in the conflict.

First, to the people and Government of South Vietnam: By your courage, by your sacrifice, you have won the precious right to determine your own future and you have developed the strength to defend that right. We look forward to working with you in the future – friends in peace as we have been allies in war.

To the leaders of North Vietnam: As we have ended the war through negotiations, let us now build a peace of reconciliation. For our part, we are prepared to make a major effort to help achieve that goal. But just as reciprocity was needed to end the war, so too will it be needed to build and strengthen the peace.

To the other major powers that have been involved even indirectly: Now is the time for mutual restraint so that the peace we have achieved can last.

And finally, to all of you who are listening, the American people: Your steadfastness in supporting our insistence on peace with honor has made peace with honor possible ...

Now that we have achieved an honorable agreement, let us be proud that America did not settle for a peace that would have betrayed our allies, that would have abandoned our prisoners of war, or that would have ended the war for us but would have continued the war for the 50 million people of Indochina. Let us be proud of the 2 1/2 million young Americans who served in Vietnam, who served with honor and distinction in one of the most selfless enterprises in the history of nations. And let us be proud of those who sacrificed, who gave their lives so that the people of South Vietnam might live in freedom and so that the world might live in peace.

In particular, I would like to say a word to some of the bravest people I have ever met – the wives, the children, the families of our prisoners of war and the missing in action. When others called on us to settle on any terms, you had the courage to stand for the right kind of peace so that those who died and those who suffered would not have died and suffered in vain, and so that where this generation knew war, the next generation would know peace. Nothing means more to me at this moment than the fact that your long vigil is coming to an end.

...

Document 38

Telephone Conversation about Chile
President Richard M. Nixon and Henry Kissinger
September 16, 1973

The election of socialist Salvador Allende as president of Chile in 1970 greatly worried the U.S. government. President Richard Nixon told U.S. Secretary of State William Rogers and National Security Adviser Henry Kissinger that he wanted Allende removed from power (Document 35). For the next three years, the United States spent $8 million trying to undermine Allende's government, which had nationalized Chile's foreign-owned copper mines and had re-established ties with Cuban communist leader Fidel Castro. Kissinger and other national security officials also encouraged Allende's rivals and leaders of the Chilean military to take action against Allende, an action consistent with some of the guidelines laid out in NSC 5412/2 (Document 16).

The coup, carried out on September 11, 1973, which the United States knew about and did not discourage, was violent. The Chilean Presidential Palace was bombed and Allende committed suicide. The Army Chief of Staff, General Augusto Pinochet, led the coup and took power. Pinochet was firmly anti-communist but also intolerant of dissent. His military regime, in power until 1990, rounded up suspected opponents. The regime killed more than 3,000 Chileans and jailed and tortured almost 30,000 more. Because of Pinochet's stance on communism, however, the U.S. government sent Chile almost $350 million in economic aid from 1973-1976. Revelations of the Pinochet regime's human rights violations did cause controversy in the United States. In part because of the U.S. role in Chile's coup, President Jimmy Carter would try to give the protection of human rights a more prominent place in U.S. foreign relations during the Cold War (Document 40). Pinochet's government liberalized the Chilean economy, which became one of the best performing economies in Latin America during the 1990s. According to the 2016 United Nations Human Development Report, Chile had the highest human development index in Latin America.

Source: National Security Archive, Electronic Briefing Book no. 255 (September 10, 2008). Available at https://goo.gl/LVaygk.

[Kissinger]: Hello.

[Nixon]: Hi, Henry.

[Kissinger]: Mr. President.

[Nixon]: Where are you. In New York?

[Kissinger]: No, I am in Washington. I am working. I may go to the football game this afternoon if I get through.

[Nixon]: Good. Good. Well it is the opener. It is better than television. Nothing new of any importance or is there?

[Kissinger]: Nothing of very great consequence. The Chilean thing is getting consolidated and of course the newspapers [are] bleeding because a pro-Communist government has been overthrown.

[Nixon]: Isn't that something. Isn't that something.

[Kissinger]: I mean instead of celebrating – in the Eisenhower period we would be heroes.

[Nixon]: Well we didn't – as you know – our hand doesn't show on this one though.

[Kissinger]: We didn't do it. I mean we helped them. _____ [blank in original] created the conditions as great as possible(? ?)

[Nixon]: That is right. And that is the way it is going to be played. But listen, as far as people are concerned let me say they aren't going to buy this crap from the Liberals on this one.

[Kissinger]: Absolutely not.

[Nixon]: They know it is a pro-Communist government and that is the way it is.

[Kissinger]: Exactly. And pro-Castro.

[Nixon]: Well the main thing was. Let's forget the pro-Communists. It was an anti-American government all the way.

[Kissinger]: Oh, wildly. . . .

[Nixon]: . . . it is just typical of the crap we are up against.

[Kissinger]: And the unbelievable filthy hypocrisy.

[Nixon]: We know that.

[Kissinger]: Of these people. When it is South Africa, if we don't overthrow them there they are raising hell.[1]

[Nixon]: Yes, that is right.

[Kissinger]: But otherwise things are fairly quiet. The Chinese are making very friendly noises. I think they are just waiting for my confirmation to make a proposal.

[Nixon]: When you say their noises are friendly, what do you mean?

---

[1] A reference to criticism of South Africa's government, which maintained a strict racial segregation policy known as apartheid.

[Kissinger]: Well their newspapers have stopped attacking us. They are blasting the Russians like crazy. . . .

[Nixon]: That is good.

[Kissinger]: You know that they wouldn't do unless they wanted to ingratiate themselves.

[Nixon]: Right, right. . . .

Document 39

Meeting on Cuba

Washington Special Actions Group

March 24, 1976

Fidel Castro, the communist Cuban dictator, remained a thorn in the side of the United States long after the resolution of the 1962 Cuban Missile Crisis (Documents 23–26). In late 1975, Castro deployed 36,000 Cuban troops to the war-torn African nation of Angola to support its newly installed communist government. For its part, the United States supported anti-communist factions fighting to take power. Angola's civil war, sparked by the abrupt withdrawal of Portugal (which had long held Angola as a colony), was thus viewed by the democratic and communist sides as an important Cold War battleground.

In the document below, numerous high-ranking security officials in the Ford administration discuss what to do in response to Cuba's action. The discussion reveals recurring Cold War problems and policies: the spread of communism globally (in this case, in Africa); the continuing goal of the United States to remove communism from Cuba; the strong preference for military action; and the need of the United States to appear strong and effective in the eyes of the world. As Kissinger commented at the end of the meeting, "[if] It looks like we can't do anything about a country of 8 million people [Angola], then in three or four years we are going to have a real crisis."

Source: National Security Archive, Electronic Briefing Book no. 487 (October 1, 2014). Available at https://goo.gl/PNox4P.

Time and Place: 10:48 a.m. – 11:10 a.m., White House Situation Room

Subject: Cuba

Participants:

Chairman: Henry A. Kissinger

[State Department]: Robert Ingersoll

[Defense Department]:   Donald Rumsfeld
                          William Clements

[Joint Chiefs of Staff]: Gen. George S. Brown

[Central Intelligence Agency]: Lt. Gen. Vernon Walters

[National Security Council]: Lt. Gen. Brent Scowcroft . . .[1]

Secretary Kissinger: Today we are going to discuss two subjects – Cuba and Lebanon. Cuba will be first. We want to get planning started in the political, economic and military fields so that we can see what we can do if we want to move against Cuba. We should get a range of options. Later there will be an NSC Meeting to discuss our objectives. Now we have to look at our capabilities so that the President [*Gerald Ford*] can make a political decision of what to do, and how to plan it. This should be done in such a way as to minimize the danger of leaks. So far in State there has been no planning.

Gen. Brown: In doing this it might be helpful to narrow the alternatives and look at one or two alternative courses.

Secretary Rumsfeld: Are you talking in terms of military planning?

Secretary Kissinger: There are a number of things that we can do which should be looked at. In the military field there is an invasion or blockade.

Secretary Rumsfeld: The other thing that should be considered is the effect this would have on our relations with the Soviet Union.

Secretary Kissinger: Right and that is the reason for our current threatening noises.

Gen. Walters: [*response blacked out*]

Gen. Brown: I don't understand. I thought there already was a working group paper that had looked at a number of options.

Secretary Kissinger: What I am talking about is a planning group with a very restricted number of people. The members of the group would be at a reasonably high level so that we can avoid horrible platitudes in the paper. This is serious business. A blockade could lead us into a confrontation with the USSR.

Secretary Rumsfeld: We should lay out our political goals regarding Cuba and Africa and then focus in on them. There are an infinite number of things we can list of a political, military [*words blacked out*] nature which would affect Cuba's position in Africa. How you do these things depends on your goals in Africa.

---

[1] Henry Kissinger was the Secretary of State and Robert Ingersoll was Deputy Secretary of State. William Clements was the Deputy Secretary of Defense; General George S. Brown was the Chairman of the Joint Chiefs of Staff; Lt. General Vernon Walters was the Deputy Director of the Central Intelligence Agency; and Lt. General Brent Scowcroft was the head of the National Security Council.

Secretary Kissinger: That is not necessarily so. The President may not want to or be able to carry out a plan just because he has one.

Mr. Clements: I am appalled at the way Cuban military forces are being used overseas. Are we just going to sit here and do nothing.

Secretary Kissinger: That is not for this group to decide. Those questions will be discussed at a full meeting of the NSC. Rhodesia is a lousy case but it is not the only problem of its kind in southern Africa. If the Cubans destroy Rhodesia then Namibia is next and then there is South Africa.[2] It might take only five years and the South Africans just won't yield. They are stubborn like the Israelis. The problem is that no matter how we build our policy in southern Africa anything that happens will appear to have resulted from Cuban pressure. We could make it a proposition that it is unacceptable to us to have the Cubans as the shock troops of the revolution. . . . This is a strategic problem regardless of our African policy. During my South American trip the President of Colombia arranged a small private dinner meeting. There were just four of us. We talked about Cuban intervention in Africa and he said he was frightened about the possibility of a race war. This could cause trouble in the Caribbean with the Cubans appealing to disaffected minorities and could then spillover into South America and even into our own country.

Secretary Rumsfeld: How do you prevent Cuba from doing that?

Secretary Kissinger: You deter them from even trying it. We must get it into the heads of the leaders of African countries that they can't have it both ways. They can't have both the Cubans in Africa and our support. It was the same situation we had with Egypt a few years ago. I told them they could not have both the Soviet presence and our support and now the Soviets have left. We have to know what we want to do. We should consider two or three likely courses of action and go into them in detail and see what problems would result. We don't necessarily have to consider an invasion but we should look at various forms of blockade.

Gen. Scowcroft: This would be a two step process. There are a variety of things like an invasion which could be ruled out.

(11:01 a.m. Secretary Rumsfeld left the meeting for another appointment.)

Secretary Kissinger: I would hate to have to implement operations against Cuba as a reaction to some event. It should be well planned. George (Brown), you should pick two or three types of operations. If we decide to use military power it must succeed. There should be no half way measures – we would get no award for using military power in moderation. If we decide on a blockade it must be ruthless and rapid and efficient.

---

[2] Rhodesia (now called Zimbabwe) and Namibia are nations in southern Africa.

Gen. Brown: I agree. There is of course the Congressional angle. There is no sense in taking a course of action unless it can be completed in less than 60 days.[3] There is no sense in starting an operation unless it can achieve its objectives quickly.

Secretary Kissinger: The President must know what would be involved in a blockade and what impact it would have on Cuba and the USSR.

Gen. Scowcroft: And Congress.

Secretary Kissinger: One thing that might be considered is a selective blockade, a blockade on outgoing stuff from Cuba and not on incoming items, except for purely economic things.

Gen. Brown: That was the sort of thing we did during the Cuban missile crisis. It was a quarantine involving only Soviet ships. One of the problems of just having a blockade on outgoing things is that most of the military equipment they are using in Africa comes directly from the Soviet Union.

Secretary Kissinger: That is the sort of thing we have to study. This is not the place to make a decision. If there is a perception overseas that we are so weakened by our internal debate so that it looks like we can't do anything about a country of 8 million people, then in three or four years we are going to have a real crisis. It is important to get public support. . . .

---

[3] Brown refers to the War Powers Act (1973) by which Congress, in response to the war in Vietnam, restricted the president's ability to commit American forces overseas without the consent of Congress. According to the act, the president must notify Congress within 48 hours of the commitment of U.S. forces abroad, and those forces cannot remain for more than 60 days unless Congress authorizes them to stay longer.

Document 40

Address at Commencement Exercises at the University of Notre Dame

President Jimmy Carter

May 22, 1977

In the document below, President Jimmy Carter outlined his plan to reinvent U.S. foreign policy by ending containment (Documents 1–2 and 6) that put an emphasis on the use of military force and covert action. Asking what is our "essential character as a nation," he answered that the United States must make international human rights a priority. Despite his criticism of certain Cold War practices, Carter made it clear that the United States was still determined to prevent the spread of communism. Indeed, Carter and his administration believed that the promotion of human rights offered an opportunity to discredit the Soviet Union for the oppression of its own citizens.

During his presidency, Carter struggled to meet the high ideals set forth in this speech. Continued support for Iran, for example, kept the United States close to a ruler, Mohammad Reza Shah, who was a flagrant violator of human rights in his nation. (He brutally suppressed political opposition and was ousted from power in 1979.) In 1979, however, Carter achieved one of his top goals: the brokering of a Middle East peace agreement that greatly improved relations between Egypt and Israel.

Source: Public Papers of the Presidents of the United States: Jimmy Carter, 1977, *Book I (Washington, D.C.: U.S. Government Printing Office, 1977), 954–62. Available online from Gerhard Peters and John T. Woolley, The American Presidency Project. https://goo.gl/UQAdCx.*

. . . I want to speak to you today about the strands that connect our actions overseas with our essential character as a nation. I believe we can have a foreign policy that is democratic, that is based on fundamental values, and that uses power and influence, which we have, for humane purposes. We can also have a foreign policy that the American people both support and, for a change, know about and understand.

I have a quiet confidence in our own political system. Because we know that democracy works, we can reject the arguments of those rulers who deny human rights to their people.

We are confident that democracy's example will be compelling, and so we seek to bring that example closer to those from whom in the past few years we have been separated and who are not yet convinced about the advantages of our kind of life.

We are confident that the democratic methods are the most effective, and so we are not tempted to employ improper tactics here at home or abroad.

We are confident of our own strength, so we can seek substantial mutual reductions in the nuclear arms race.

And we are confident of the good sense of American people, and so we let them share in the process of making foreign policy decisions. We can thus speak with the voices of 215 million, and not just of an isolated handful.

Democracy's great recent successes – in India, Portugal, Spain, Greece[1] – show that our confidence in this system is not misplaced. Being confident of our own future, we are now free of that inordinate fear of communism which once led us to embrace any dictator who joined us in that fear. I'm glad that that's being changed.

For too many years, we've been willing to adopt the flawed and erroneous principles and tactics of our adversaries, sometimes abandoning our own values for theirs. We've fought fire with fire, never thinking that fire is better quenched with water. This approach failed, with Vietnam the best example of its intellectual and moral poverty. But through failure we have now found our way back to our own principles and values, and we have regained our lost confidence.

By the measure of history, our Nation's 200 years are very brief, and our rise to world eminence is briefer still. It dates from 1945, when Europe and the old international order lay in ruins. Before then, America was largely on the periphery of world affairs. But since then, we have inescapably been at the center of world affairs.

Our policy during this period was guided by two principles: a belief that Soviet expansion was almost inevitable but that it must be contained, and the corresponding belief in the importance of an almost exclusive alliance among non-Communist nations on both sides of the Atlantic. That system could not last forever unchanged. Historical trends have weakened its foundation. The unifying threat of conflict with the Soviet Union has become less intensive, even though the competition has become more extensive.

---

[1] A state of emergency in India, during which elections were suspended, had ended after 21 months in March 1977. Portugal, Spain, and Greece had recently returned to democratic governance.

The Vietnamese war produced a profound moral crisis, sapping worldwide faith in our own policy and our system of life, a crisis of confidence made even more grave by the covert pessimism of some of our leaders.

In less than a generation, we've seen the world change dramatically. The daily lives and aspirations of most human beings have been transformed. Colonialism is nearly gone. A new sense of national identity now exists in almost 100 new countries that have been formed in the last generation. Knowledge has become more widespread. Aspirations are higher. As more people have been freed from traditional constraints, more have been determined to achieve, for the first time in their lives, social justice.

The world is still divided by ideological disputes, dominated by regional conflicts, and threatened by danger that we will not resolve the differences of race and wealth without violence or without drawing into combat the major military powers. We can no longer separate the traditional issues of war and peace from the new global questions of justice, equity, and human rights.

It is a new world, but America should not fear it. It is a new world, and we should help to shape it. It is a new world that calls for a new American foreign policy – a policy based on constant decency in its values and on optimism in our historical vision.

We can no longer have a policy solely for the industrial nations as the foundation of global stability, but we must respond to the new reality of a politically awakening world.

We can no longer expect that the other 150 nations will follow the dictates of the powerful, but we must continue – confidently – our efforts to inspire, to persuade, and to lead.

Our policy must reflect our belief that the world can hope for more than simple survival and our belief that dignity and freedom are fundamental spiritual requirements. Our policy must shape an international system that will last longer than secret deals.

We cannot make this kind of policy by manipulation. Our policy must be open; it must be candid; it must be one of constructive global involvement . . . .

. . . [W]e have reaffirmed America's commitment to human rights as a fundamental tenet of our foreign policy. In ancestry, religion, color, place of origin, and cultural background, we Americans are as diverse a nation as the world has even seen. No common mystique of blood or soil unites us. What draws us together, perhaps more than anything else, is a belief in human freedom. We want the world to know that our Nation stands for more than financial prosperity.

This does not mean that we can conduct our foreign policy by rigid moral maxims. We live in a world that is imperfect and which will always be imperfect

– a world that is complex and confused and which will always be complex and confused.

I understand fully the limits of moral suasion. We have no illusion that changes will come easily or soon. But I also believe that it is a mistake to undervalue the power of words and of the ideas that words embody. In our own history, that power has ranged from Thomas Paine's "Common Sense" to Martin Luther King, Jr.'s "I Have a Dream."

In the life of the human spirit, words are action, much more so than many of us may realize who live in countries where freedom of expression is taken for granted. The leaders of totalitarian nations understand this very well. The proof is that words are precisely the action for which dissidents in those countries are being persecuted.

Nonetheless, we can already see dramatic, worldwide advances in the protection of the individual from the arbitrary power of the state. For us to ignore this trend would be to lose influence and moral authority in the world. To lead it will be to regain the moral stature that we once had.

The great democracies are not free because we are strong and prosperous. I believe we are strong and influential and prosperous because we are free.

Throughout the world today, in free nations and in totalitarian countries as well, there is a preoccupation with the subject of human freedom, human rights. And I believe it is incumbent on us in this country to keep that discussion, that debate, that contention alive. No other country is as well-qualified as we to set an example. We have our own shortcomings and faults, and we should strive constantly and with courage to make sure that we are legitimately proud of what we have. . . .

. . . [W]e've moved to engage the Soviet Union in a joint effort to halt the strategic arms race. This race is not only dangerous, it's morally deplorable. We must put an end to it. . . .

. . . I believe in détente with the Soviet Union. To me it means progress toward peace. But the effects of détente should not be limited to our own two countries alone. We hope to persuade the Soviet Union that one country cannot impose its system of society upon another, either through direct military intervention or through the use of a client state's military force, as was the case with Cuban intervention in Angola. . . .

. . . [W]e are taking deliberate steps to improve the chances of lasting peace in the Middle East. Through wide-ranging consultation with leaders of the countries involved – Israel, Syria, Jordan, and Egypt – we have found some areas of agreement and some movement toward consensus. The negotiations must continue. . . .

It's important that we make progress toward normalizing relations with the People's Republic of China. We see the American and Chinese relationship as a central element of our global policy and China as a key force for global peace. We wish to cooperate closely with the creative Chinese people on the problems that confront all mankind. And we hope to find a formula which can bridge some of the difficulties that still separate us.

Finally, let me say that we are committed to a peaceful resolution of the crisis in southern Africa. The time has come for the principle of majority rule to be the basis for political order, recognizing that in a democratic system the rights of the minority must also be protected.

To be peaceful, change must come promptly. The United States is determined to work together with our European allies and with the concerned African States to shape a congenial international framework for the rapid and progressive transformation of southern African society and to help protect it from unwarranted outside interference.

Let me conclude by summarizing: Our policy is based on an historical vision of America's role. Our policy is derived from a larger view of global change. Our policy is rooted in our moral values, which never change. Our policy is reinforced by our material wealth and by our military power. Our policy is designed to serve mankind. And it is a policy that I hope will make you proud to be Americans.

Document 41

Address to the Nation on the Soviet Invasion of Afghanistan

President Jimmy Carter

January 4, 1980

In 1978, a Communist Party in Afghanistan seized power in a coup. This led to a period of civil war and infighting within the Communist Party. In late 1979, the Soviet Union sent troops into Afghanistan, with which it shared a border, in order to install a communist faction to its liking. Soviet forces soon numbered 100,000. An informal coalition known as the Mujahideen fought to oust the Soviets, resulting in a protracted war. The costs in lives and money of the occupation of Afghanistan eventually forced the Soviet Union to withdraw, although this process was not completed until early 1989. The failed intervention in Afghanistan was one element leading to the dissolution of the Soviet Union (1991).

Source: Public Papers of the Presidents of the United States: Jimmy Carter, 1980-81, *Book I (Washington, D.C.: U.S. Government Printing Office, 1981), 21–4. Available online from Gerhard Peters and John T. Woolley, The American Presidency Project. https://goo.gl/ZebFUZ.*

I come to you this evening to discuss the extremely important and rapidly changing circumstances in Southwest Asia. . . .

. . . Massive Soviet military forces have invaded the small, nonaligned, sovereign nation of Afghanistan, which had hitherto not been an occupied satellite of the Soviet Union.

Fifty thousand heavily armed Soviet troops have crossed the border and are now dispersed throughout Afghanistan, attempting to conquer the fiercely independent Muslim people of that country.

The Soviets claim, falsely, that they were invited into Afghanistan to help protect that country from some unnamed outside threat. But the President, who had been the leader of Afghanistan before the Soviet invasion, was assassinated – along with several members of his family – after the Soviets gained control of the capital city of Kabul. Only several days later was the new puppet leader even brought into Afghanistan by the Soviets.

This invasion is an extremely serious threat to peace because of the threat of further Soviet expansion into neighboring countries in Southwest Asia and also because such an aggressive military policy is unsettling to other peoples throughout the world.

This is a callous violation of international law and the United Nations Charter. It is a deliberate effort of a powerful atheistic government to subjugate an independent Islamic people.

We must recognize the strategic importance of Afghanistan to stability and peace. A Soviet-occupied Afghanistan threatens both Iran and Pakistan and is a steppingstone to possible control over much of the world's oil supplies.

The United States wants all nations in the region to be free and to be independent. If the Soviets are encouraged in this invasion by eventual success, and if they maintain their dominance over Afghanistan and then extend their control to adjacent countries, the stable, strategic, and peaceful balance of the entire world will be changed. This would threaten the security of all nations including, of course, the United States, our allies, and our friends.

Therefore, the world simply cannot stand by and permit the Soviet Union to commit this act with impunity. Fifty nations have petitioned the United Nations Security Council to condemn the Soviet Union and to demand the immediate withdrawal of all Soviet troops from Afghanistan.

... [N]either the United States nor any other nation which is committed to world peace and stability can continue to do business as usual with the Soviet Union.

I have already recalled the United States Ambassador from Moscow back to Washington. He's working with me and with my other senior advisers in an immediate and comprehensive evaluation of the whole range of our relations with the Soviet Union.

The successful negotiation of the SALT II treaty[1] has been a major goal and a major achievement of this administration, and we Americans, the people of the Soviet Union, and indeed the entire world will benefit from the successful control of strategic nuclear weapons through the implementation of this carefully negotiated treaty.

However, because of the Soviet aggression, I have asked the United States Senate to defer further consideration of the SALT II treaty so that the Congress and I can assess Soviet actions and intentions and devote our primary attention to the legislative and other measures required to respond to this crisis. As

---

[1] The Strategic Arms Limitation Treaty (SALT). The United States and the Soviet Union first signed an agreement in 1972 to limit their number of nuclear weapons. A second treaty had just been signed, but the Soviet invasion of Afghanistan resulted in the U.S. Senate not ratifying the agreement.

circumstances change in the future, we will, of course, keep the ratification of SALT II under active review in consultation with the leaders of the Senate.

The Soviets must understand our deep concern. We will delay opening of any new American or Soviet consular facilities, and most of the cultural and economic exchanges currently under consideration will be deferred. Trade with the Soviet Union will be severely restricted. . . .

Along with other countries, we will provide military equipment, food, and other assistance to help Pakistan defend its independence and its national security against the seriously increased threat it now faces from the north. The United States also stands ready to help other nations in the region in similar ways.

Neither our allies nor our potential adversaries should have the slightest doubt about our willingness, our determination, and our capacity to take the measures I have outlined tonight. I have consulted with leaders of the Congress, and I am confident they will support legislation that may be required to carry out these measures.

History teaches, perhaps, very few clear lessons. But surely one such lesson learned by the world at great cost is that aggression, unopposed, becomes a contagious disease. . . .

Document 42

Address to the Nation on Defense and National Security

President Ronald Reagan

March 23, 1983

Ronald Reagan ran for president in 1980 promising to increase defense spending. He was elected in part because the Soviet invasion of Afghanistan (Document 41), Cuban operations in Africa, the seizure of the American Embassy in Tehran (November 1979), and the subsequent holding of American diplomats as hostages convinced at least some voters that America had become dangerously weak. A long-time critic of détente (Document 36), Reagan came into office hoping to end the Cold War with a victory for the United States by peacefully causing the collapse of communism in Eastern Europe and even in the Soviet Union. A key element of his strategy was a military buildup, undertaken, as he explained in this speech, because, as the example of World War II showed, weakness encouraged war.

Reagan recounted (in passages omitted from this excerpt) evidence of increases in the quantity and quality of Soviet weapons. He also used photographs to illustrate the results of aggressive Soviet actions close to America, including a large Soviet intelligence-gathering facility in Cuba, Soviet military equipment in Nicaragua, and a large Cuban-built airfield on the Caribbean island of Grenada. Reagan then turned to his primary topic – encouraging support for his administration's defense plans and spending. An important departure in these plans was an expensive and experimental defensive weapons project known as the Strategic Defense Initiative (often also called "Star Wars" after the popular 1978 film of the same name). The SDI was a plan to build a network of space- and earth-based lasers with the capability to target intercontinental ballistic missiles (ICBMs) fired at the United States. Reagan presented this initiative as a decisive break with the long-standing Cold War deterrence strategy of mutually assured destruction, in which each side possessing nuclear weapons was assured or secured by the knowledge that any use of nuclear weapons would lead to the destruction of the country that used them. In theory, this mutually assured destruction meant nuclear weapons would never be used. Reagan believed that rendering nuclear weapons unusable through an effective defense against them was a surer way of putting an end to the possibility of nuclear war.

Reagan succeeded in obtaining Congressional funding for SDI, but the system was not completed during his presidency. Research and development continued leading to the development of some anti-missile weapons, but as yet an operable SDI has not been built.

Source: Public Papers of the Presidents of the United States: Ronald Reagan, 1983, *Book I (Washington, D.C.: U.S. Government Printing Office, 1984),* 437–43. *Available online from Gerhard Peters and John T. Woolley,* The American Presidency Project. *https://goo.gl/2uDvaG.*

My fellow Americans, thank you for sharing your time with me tonight.

The subject I want to discuss with you, peace and national security, is both timely and important. Timely, because I've reached a decision which offers a new hope for our children in the 21st century, a decision I'll tell you about in a few minutes. And important because there's a very big decision that you must make for yourselves. This subject involves the most basic duty that any President and any people share, the duty to protect and strengthen the peace.

. . .

The budget request that is now before the Congress has been trimmed to the limits of safety. Further deep cuts cannot be made without seriously endangering the security of the Nation. The choice is up to the men and women you've elected to the Congress, and that means the choice is up to you.

Tonight, I want to explain to you what this defense debate is all about and why I'm convinced that the budget now before the Congress is necessary, responsible, and deserving of your support. And I want to offer hope for the future.

But first, let me say what the defense debate is not about. It is not about spending arithmetic. . . .

What seems to have been lost in all this debate is the simple truth of how a defense budget is arrived at. It isn't done by deciding to spend a certain number of dollars. . . .

There is no logical way that you can say, let's spend x billion dollars less. You can only say, which part of our defense measures do we believe we can do without and still have security against all contingencies? . . .

The defense policy of the United States is based on a simple premise: The United States does not start fights. We will never be an aggressor. We maintain our strength in order to deter and defend against aggression-to preserve freedom and peace. . . .

This strategy of deterrence has not changed. It still works. But what it takes to maintain deterrence has changed. It took one kind of military force to deter an attack when we had far more nuclear weapons than any other power; it takes another kind now that the Soviets, for example, have enough accurate and powerful nuclear weapons to destroy virtually all of our missiles on the ground. Now, this is not to say that the Soviet Union is planning to make war on us. Nor do I believe a war is inevitable – quite the contrary. But what must be recognized is that our security is based on being prepared to meet all threats.

. . .

The calls for cutting back the defense budget come in nice, simple arithmetic. They're the same kind of talk that led the democracies to neglect their defenses in the 1930's and invited the tragedy of World War II. We must not let that grim chapter of history repeat itself through apathy or neglect.

This is why I'm speaking to you tonight – to urge you to tell your Senators and Congressmen that you know we must continue to restore our military strength. If we stop in midstream, we will send a signal of decline, of lessened will, to friends and adversaries alike. Free people must voluntarily, through open debate and democratic means, meet the challenge that totalitarians pose by compulsion. It's up to us, in our time, to choose and choose wisely between the hard but necessary task of preserving peace and freedom and the temptation to ignore our duty and blindly hope for the best while the enemies of freedom grow stronger day by day.

The solution is well within our grasp. But to reach it, there is simply no alternative but to continue this year, in this budget, to provide the resources we need to preserve the peace and guarantee our freedom.

Now, thus far tonight I've shared with you my thoughts on the problems of national security we must face together. My predecessors in the Oval Office have appeared before you on other occasions to describe the threat posed by Soviet power and have proposed steps to address that threat. But since the advent of nuclear weapons, those steps have been increasingly directed toward deterrence of aggression through the promise of retaliation.

This approach to stability through offensive threat has worked. We and our allies have succeeded in preventing nuclear war for more than three decades. In recent months, however, my advisers, including in particular the Joint Chiefs of Staff, have underscored the necessity to break out of a future that relies solely on offensive retaliation for our security.

Over the course of these discussions, I've become more and more deeply convinced that the human spirit must be capable of rising above dealing with other nations and human beings by threatening their existence. Feeling this way, I believe we must thoroughly examine every opportunity for reducing tensions and for introducing greater stability into the strategic calculus on both sides.

One of the most important contributions we can make is, of course, to lower the level of all arms, and particularly nuclear arms. We're engaged right now in several negotiations with the Soviet Union to bring about a mutual reduction of weapons. I will report to you a week from tomorrow my thoughts on that score. But let me just say, I'm totally committed to this course.

If the Soviet Union will join with us in our effort to achieve major arms reduction, we will have succeeded in stabilizing the nuclear balance. Nevertheless, it will still be necessary to rely on the specter of retaliation, on mutual threat. And that's a sad commentary on the human condition. Wouldn't it be better to save lives than to avenge them? Are we not capable of demonstrating our peaceful intentions by applying all our abilities and our ingenuity to achieving a truly lasting stability? I think we are. Indeed, we must.

After careful consultation with my advisers, including the Joint Chiefs of Staff, I believe there is a way. Let me share with you a vision of the future which offers hope. It is that we embark on a program to counter the awesome Soviet missile threat with measures that are defensive. Let us turn to the very strengths in technology that spawned our great industrial base and that have given us the quality of life we enjoy today.

What if free people could live secure in the knowledge that their security did not rest upon the threat of instant U.S. retaliation to deter a Soviet attack, that we could intercept and destroy strategic ballistic missiles before they reached our own soil or that of our allies?

I know this is a formidable, technical task, one that may not be accomplished before the end of this century.

Yet, current technology has attained a level of sophistication where it's reasonable for us to begin this effort. It will take years, probably decades of effort on many fronts. There will be failures and setbacks, just as there will be successes and breakthroughs. And as we proceed, we must remain constant in preserving the nuclear deterrent and maintaining a solid capability for flexible response. But isn't it worth every investment necessary to free the world from the threat of nuclear war? We know it is.

In the meantime, we will continue to pursue real reductions in nuclear arms, negotiating from a position of strength that can be ensured only by modernizing our strategic forces. At the same time, we must take steps to reduce the risk of a conventional military conflict escalating to nuclear war by improving our nonnuclear capabilities.

America does possess – now – the technologies to attain very significant improvements in the effectiveness of our conventional, nonnuclear forces. Proceeding boldly with these new technologies, we can significantly reduce any incentive that the Soviet Union may have to threaten attack against the United States or its allies.

As we pursue our goal of defensive technologies, we recognize that our allies rely upon our strategic offensive power to deter attacks against them. Their vital interests and ours are inextricably linked. Their safety and ours are one. And no change in technology can or will alter that reality. We must and shall continue to honor our commitments.

I clearly recognize that defensive systems have limitations and raise certain problems and ambiguities. If paired with offensive systems, they can be viewed as fostering an aggressive policy, and no one wants that. But with these considerations firmly in mind, I call upon the scientific community in our country, those who gave us nuclear weapons, to turn their great talents now to the cause of mankind and world peace, to give us the means of rendering these nuclear weapons impotent and obsolete.

Tonight, consistent with our obligations of the ABM treaty[1] and recognizing the need for closer consultation with our allies, I'm taking an important first step. I am directing a comprehensive and intensive effort to define a long-term research and development program to begin to achieve our ultimate goal of eliminating the threat posed by strategic nuclear missiles. This could pave the way for arms control measures to eliminate the weapons themselves. We seek neither military superiority nor political advantage. Our only purpose – one all people share – is to search for ways to reduce the danger of nuclear war.

My fellow Americans, tonight we're launching an effort which holds the promise of changing the course of human history. There will be risks, and results take time. But I believe we can do it. As we cross this threshold, I ask for your prayers and your support.

---

[1] The Anti-Ballistic Missile Treaty (1972–2002) between the United States and the Soviet Union limited what each party could do to defend against ballistic missiles.

Document 43

Remarks on East-West Relations at the Brandenburg Gate in West Berlin

President Ronald Reagan

June 12, 1987

In 1987, President Ronald Reagan delivered a speech in West Berlin within sight of the Berlin Wall. Since its erection in 1961, the wall had both symbolized and entrenched the division between communist and democratic Europe. As Reagan noted, John F. Kennedy was the first U.S. president to speak to West Berliners (Document 27). Reagan went much further than Kennedy in criticizing the wall. In the most memorable line from the speech, Reagan urged the leader of the Soviet Union, Mikhail Gorbachev, to "Tear down this wall!" State Department advisors had counseled the president not to make this statement, believing it to be needlessly provocative. It was important to Reagan, however, to point out the reason for the wall's construction and continued existence: Soviet domination of the communist states in Europe, including East Germany.

Source: Public Papers of the Presidents of the United States: Ronald Reagan, 1987, Book I (Washington, D.C.: U.S. Government Printing Office, 1989), 634–8. Available online from Gerhard Peters and John T. Woolley, The American Presidency Project. https://goo.gl/hPdkkc.

. . . Twenty-four years ago, President John F. Kennedy visited Berlin, speaking to the people of this city and the world at the city hall. Well, since then two other presidents have come, each in his turn, to Berlin. And today I, myself, make my second visit to your city.

We come to Berlin, we American Presidents, because it's our duty to speak, in this place, of freedom. . . .

Behind me stands a wall that encircles the free sectors of this city, part of a vast system of barriers that divides the entire continent of Europe. From the Baltic, south, those barriers cut across Germany in a gash of barbed wire, concrete, dog runs, and guard towers. Farther south, there may be no visible, no obvious wall. But there remain armed guards and checkpoints all the same – still a restriction on the right to travel, still an instrument to impose upon ordinary men and women the will of a totalitarian state. Yet it is here in Berlin where the wall emerges most clearly; here, cutting across your city, where the news photo and the television screen have imprinted this brutal division of a continent upon the mind of the world. Standing before the Brandenburg Gate,[1] every man is a German, separated from his fellow men. Every man is a Berliner, forced to look upon a scar.

... Today I say: As long as this gate is closed, as long as this scar of a wall is permitted to stand, it is not the German question alone that remains open, but the question of freedom for all mankind. Yet I do not come here to lament. For I find in Berlin a message of hope, even in the shadow of this wall, a message of triumph.

In this season of spring in 1945, the people of Berlin emerged from their air-raid shelters to find devastation. Thousands of miles away, the people of the United States reached out to help. And in 1947 Secretary of State – as you've been told – George Marshall announced the creation of what would become known as the Marshall plan.[2] Speaking precisely 40 years ago this month, he said: "Our policy is directed not against any country or doctrine, but against hunger, poverty, desperation, and chaos."

In the Reichstag a few moments ago, I saw a display commemorating this 40th anniversary of the Marshall plan. I was struck by the sign on a burnt-out, gutted structure that was being rebuilt. I understand that Berliners of my own generation can remember seeing signs like it dotted throughout the Western sectors of the city. The sign read simply: "The Marshall plan is helping here to strengthen the free world." A strong, free world in the West, that dream became real. Japan rose from ruin to become an economic giant. Italy, France, Belgium – virtually every nation in Western Europe saw political and economic rebirth; the European Community was founded.

In West Germany and here in Berlin, there took place an economic miracle
....

... From devastation, from utter ruin, you Berliners have, in freedom, rebuilt a city that once again ranks as one of the greatest on Earth. ...

In the 1950's, Khrushchev predicted: "We will bury you."[3] But in the West today, we see a free world that has achieved a level of prosperity and well-being

---

[1] The Berlin Wall passed within yards of the historic Brandenburg Gate at the foot of one of Berlin's major avenues, offering a striking backdrop to the divided city. Reagan spoke on the western side of the gate.

[2] See Document 3.

[3] In 1956 in Moscow, Soviet leader Nikita Khrushchev told ambassadors from non-communist nations that communism would "dig you in," a phrase that was translated in English language media as "we will bury you."

unprecedented in all human history. In the Communist world, we see failure, technological backwardness, declining standards of health, even want of the most basic kind – too little food. Even today, the Soviet Union still cannot feed itself. After these four decades, then, there stands before the entire world one great and inescapable conclusion: Freedom leads to prosperity. Freedom replaces the ancient hatreds among the nations with comity and peace. Freedom is the victor.

And now the Soviets themselves may, in a limited way, be coming to understand the importance of freedom. We hear much from Moscow about a new policy of reform and openness. Some political prisoners have been released. Certain foreign news broadcasts are no longer being jammed. Some economic enterprises have been permitted to operate with greater freedom from state control. Are these the beginnings of profound changes in the Soviet state? Or are they token gestures, intended to raise false hopes in the West, or to strengthen the Soviet system without changing it? We welcome change and openness; for we believe that freedom and security go together, that the advance of human liberty can only strengthen the cause of world peace.

There is one sign the Soviets can make that would be unmistakable, that would advance dramatically the cause of freedom and peace. General Secretary Gorbachev, if you seek peace, if you seek prosperity for the Soviet Union and Eastern Europe, if you seek liberalization: Come here to this gate! Mr. Gorbachev, open this gate! Mr. Gorbachev, tear down this wall!

I understand the fear of war and the pain of division that afflict this continent – and I pledge to you my country's efforts to help overcome these burdens....

In Europe, only one nation and those it controls refuse to join the community of freedom. Yet in this age of redoubled economic growth, of information and innovation, the Soviet Union faces a choice: It must make fundamental changes, or it will become obsolete. Today thus represents a moment of hope. We in the West stand ready to cooperate with the East to promote true openness, to break down barriers that separate people, to create a safer, freer world.

And surely there is no better place than Berlin, the meeting place of East and West, to make a start....

Document 44

National Security Directive 23, "United States Relations with the Soviet Union"
National Security Council
September 22, 1989

In the mid-1980s, Soviet leader Mikhail Gorbachev introduced reforms that eased some restrictions on political speech (glasnost) and state control of the economy (perestroika). He also reduced Soviet control over Eastern Europe. Gorbachev did not intend his reforms to be steps toward democratization; indeed, he hoped glasnost *and* perestroika *would actually strengthen communism by convincing the Soviet people that the regime could adapt and improve. These reforms attracted the skeptical attention of U.S. leaders and national security officials. In setting out guidelines for a possible transition to a post-Cold War world, National Security Directive 23 (NSD 23) expressed this skepticism, demanding that Soviet actions live up to Gorbachev's words. NSD 23 may be seen as a sequel to NSC 68, the 1950 policy paper that set durable guidelines for U.S. Cold War actions (Document 6). In its call for vigilance, NSD 23 also echoed George Kennan's Long Telegram of 1946 (Document 1). NSD 23 reinforced a long-standing Cold War policy: the United States must promote democratic values and forces, not as a provocation, but to create a better relationship with the Soviets and to fulfill the long-term U.S. aim of globally promoting democracy and its values. This meant, however, that while NSD 23 required that the Soviet Union not meddle in the internal affairs of other countries, the United States would meddle in the Soviet Union's by requiring that it adopt a market economy and a democratic political system as a prerequisite for "a new cooperative relationship between Moscow and the West."*

Less than two months after President George H. W. Bush signed this directive, the "new era" came with remarkable suddenness. The Berlin Wall fell and a path to German unification opened, one the Soviet Union did not block. Poland continued its peaceful transformation from communism, as did Hungary and Czechoslovakia. The collapse of communism and its replacement with democratic forms of government and capitalism, the long-term goal of the United States, was now fully under way. A top priority for the United States was to ensure that these seismic changes did not cause instability or war in Europe.

Source: National Security Archive, Electronic Briefing Book no. 293 (November 7, 2009). Available at https://goo.gl/PNLfRA.

For forty years the United States has committed its power and will to containing the military and ideological threat of Soviet communism. Containment was never an end in itself; it was a strategy born of the conditions of the postwar world. The United States recognized that, while Soviet military power was not the only threat to international stability, it was the most immediate and grave one. The U.S. challenge was to prevent the spread of Soviet communism while rebuilding the economic, political, and social strength of the world's long-standing and new democracies. Those who crafted the strategy of containment also believed that the Soviet Union, denied the course of external expansion, would ultimately have to face and react to the internal contradictions of its own inefficient repressive and inhumane system.

This strategy provided an enduring pillar for the growth of Western democracy and free enterprise. While the most important goal of containment has been met – the development of free and prosperous societies in Western Europe and in other parts of the world – the Soviet military threat has not diminished. Rather, in the last two decades, the Soviet Union has increased its military power across the spectrum of capabilities, drawing on that power to exacerbate local conflicts and to conduct a global foreign policy opposed to Western interests. The Soviet Union has stood apart from the internal order and often worked to undermine it.

The character of the changes taking place in the Soviet Union leads to the possibility that a new era may be now upon us. We may be able to move beyond containment to a U.S. policy that actively promotes the integration of the Soviet Union into the existing international system. The U.S.S.R. had indicated an interest in rapprochement[1] with the international order and criticized major tenets of its own postwar political-military policy.

These are words that we can only applaud. But a new relationship with the international system cannot simply be declared by Moscow. Nor can it be granted by others. It must be earned through the demilitarization of Soviet foreign policy and reinforced by behavior consistent with the principles of world order to which the Soviet Union subscribed in 1945 but has repeatedly violated since. The Soviet Union cannot enjoy the fruits of membership in the community of states while holding ideological principles and engaging in conduct that promote the overthrow of that community.

The transformation of the Soviet Union from a source of instability to a productive force within the family of nations is a long-term goal that can only be

---

[1] That is, cooperating with.

pursued from a position of American strength and with patience and creativity. Our policy is not designed to help a particular leader or set of leaders in the Soviet Union. We seek, instead, fundamental [alterations] in Soviet military force structure, institutions, and practices which can only be reversed at great cost, economically and politically, to the Soviet Union. If we succeed, the ground for cooperation will widen, while that for conflict narrows. The U.S.-Soviet relationship may still be fundamentally competitive, but it will be less militarized and safer.

We are in a period of transition and uncertainty. We will not react to reforms and changes in the Soviet Union that have not yet taken place, nor will we respond to every Soviet initiative. We will be vigilant, recognizing that the Soviet Union is still governed by authoritarian methods and that its powerful armed forces remain a threat to our security and that of our allies. But the United States will challenge the Soviet Union step by step, issue by issue and institution by institution to behave in accordance with the higher standards that the Soviet leadership itself has enunciated. Moscow will find the United States a willing partner in building a better relationship. The foundation of that relationship will grow firmer if the Soviet reforms lead to conditions that will support a new cooperative relationship between Moscow and the West. Those conditions include:

- Deployment of a Soviet force posture that is smaller and much less threatening. The United States believes that the Soviet Union has legitimate security interests but Soviet military power is far greater than that needed to defend those interests.

- Renunciation of the principle that class conflict is a source of international tension and establishment of a record of conduct consistent with that pledge.

- Adherence to the obligation that it undertook at the end of World War II to permit self-determination for the countries of East-Central Europe. Moscow must authoritatively renounce the "Brezhnev Doctrine" and reaffirm the pledge of signatories to the U.N. Charter to refrain from the threat or use of force against the territorial integrity or political independence of any state.

- Demilitarization of Soviet foreign policy in other regions of the world and serious participation in efforts to ameliorate conflict, including bringing pressure to bear on Soviet clients who do not recognize the legitimate security interests of their neighbors.

- Participation in cooperative efforts to stop the proliferation of ballistic missile technology as well as nuclear, chemical and biological weapons.

- Willingness to cooperate with the United States to address pressing global problems, including the international trade in drugs and narcotics, terrorism, and dangers to the environment.
- Institutionalization of democratic internal laws and human rights practices, political pluralism, and a more market-oriented economic structure, which will establish a firm Soviet domestic base for a more productive and cooperative relationship with the free nations of the world.

[....]

Political-Diplomatic Objectives

Regional Issues

U.S. Policy will encourage fundamental political and economic reform, including freely contested elections, in East-Central Europe ....
I [*President George H.W. Bush*] direct the Secretary of State to:

Consider the most appropriate ways to engage the Soviets in discussions on resolving regional conflicts and eliminating threatening Soviet positions of influence around the world.

Transnational

The United States and the Soviet Union share an interest in reversing the spread of drugs and narcotics. The United States must challenge the Soviet Union to refrain from directly or indirectly supporting or training terrorists and insist that its allies do the same. ....

I [*President George H.W. Bush*] also direct the Secretary of State to:

Examine ways in which the Soviet Union and the United States might cooperate on environmental issues.

The Vice President should:

Explore through the National Space Council ways that the United States and the Soviet Union might jointly use space to advance our mutual interests. A particularly promising area might be research on the environment in support of multilateral efforts to protect our planet.

[....]

Democratization

The United States is encouraged by emerging trends in the internal political processes in the Soviet Union. Our concern about the character of the Soviet system, which denies its people basic political and economic liberties and pursues a policy of expansion abroad, is at the heart of our difference with Moscow. Let no one doubt the sincerity of the American people and their government in our desire to see reform succeed inside the Soviet Union. We welcome the positive changes that have taken place and we will continue to encourage greater recognition of human rights, market incentives, and free elections. To the extent that Soviet practices are modified and institutions are built based on popular will, we may find that the nature of the threat itself has changed, though any such transformation could take decades.

Where possible, the United States should promote Western values and ideas within the Soviet Union, not in the spirit of provocation or destabilization, but as a means to lay a firm foundation for a cooperative relationship. I direct the United States Information Agency, within budgetary limitations, to find new ways to promote the flow of information about American institutions and ideals to the Soviet Union. A special effort should be made to encourage private sector initiatives in support of this objective. . . .

Conclusion

The goal of restructuring the relationship of the Soviet Union to the international system is an ambitious task. The responsibility for creating the conditions to move beyond containment to integrate the Soviet Union into the family of nations lies first and foremost with Moscow. But the United States will do its part, together with our allies, to challenge and test Soviet intentions and, while maintaining our strength, to work to place Soviet relations with the West on a firmer, more cooperative course than has heretofore been possible.

Document 45

Telephone Conversation
President George H.W. Bush and Helmut Kohl
November 10, 1989

This brief telephone conversation between Helmut Kohl, Chancellor (equivalent of prime minister) of West Germany, and U.S. President George H.W. Bush offers a glimpse into the attitudes and responses of major Western leaders as the Cold War was ending. It is particularly interesting because it took place the day after the East Germans had opened the Berlin Wall. Kohl described what was happening in Berlin and his concerns for the future.

President Bush praised Kohl for his handling of the Berlin Wall situation and promised to cooperate with efforts to help Poland. Bush also promised that U.S. leaders would avoid making provocative statements that might anger the Soviets or other communist leaders. This commitment revealed Bush's basic approach to the rapid, dramatic changes taking place: U.S. efforts to support its allies and facilitate the collapse of communism should be undertaken in such a way as to avoid a Soviet backlash.

Source: National Security Archive, Electronic Briefing Book no. 293 (November 7, 2009). Available at https://goo.gl/dY1fKq.

Chancellor Kohl: The reforms in Poland are moving ahead. They have a new government with fine people. They are too idealistic with too little professionalism. Many of their professionals have spent the last couple of years in prison, not a place where one can learn how to govern. They are committed to democracy and market economics; we must help them. My request is as follows. I just told Margaret Thatcher and will tell Mitterrand[1] tomorrow that we should give instructions to our representatives at the IMF[2] that the negotiations with Poland should be completed speedily. These negotiations are

---

[1] Margaret Thatcher was the Prime Minister of Great Britain and Francois Mitterand was the President of France; both nations were longtime allies of the United States during the Cold War.

[2] The International Monetary Fund, established at the end of World War II, is a global organization that seeks to stabilize currencies and provides loans to developing countries.

not nice for the Poles but they are aware of the need and they seek clarity and clear cut conditions. We should help to get an agreement completed by the end of November. So I ask you, help us. Go and do this in the interest of the people. With respect to the rest of my trip to Poland, I will tell you next week after I return. Do you have any questions on Poland.

The President: I have no questions. I'll be interested to hear from you next week. I'm very interested in the GDR [East Germany].

Kohl: I've just arrived from Berlin. It is like witnessing an enormous fair. It has the atmosphere of a festival. The frontiers are absolutely open. At certain points they are literally taking down the wall and building new checkpoints. At Checkpoint Charlie,[3] thousands of people are crossing both ways. There are many young people who are coming over for a visit and enjoying our open way of life. I expect they will go home tonight. I would cautiously tell you that it appears that the opening has not led to a dramatic increase in the movement of refugees. It may be with the frontier open, people will simply go back and forth, looking, visiting and going home. This will work only if the GDR really reforms and I have my doubts. Krenz[4] will carry out reforms but I think there are limits. One of those limits seems to be one party rule, and this simply will not work. Certainly, in particular, it will not work without pluralism, free trade unions and so forth. I could imagine that this will continue for a few weeks – that for a few weeks people will wait to see if the reforms come and if there is no light at the end of the tunnel they will run away from the GDR in great numbers. This would be a catastrophe for economic development; good people are leaving. The figures this year – 230,000 have come. Their average age has been between 25 and 30. This is a catastrophe for the GDR. They are doctors, lawyers, specialists who cannot be replaced. They can earn more here. This is a dramatic thing; an historic hour. Let me repeat. There were two major manifestations (political gatherings) in Berlin. One was in front of the Berlin Town Hall where there were a lot of left wing rowdies, these are the pictures that will be shown on TV around the world. The second was at the Kurfurstendamm[5] organized by our political friends. It was at about 6:30PM and the estimates are that there were 120,000 – 200,000 people. The overall spirit was optimistic and friendly. When I thanked the Americans for their role in all of this, there was much applause. Without the U.S. this day would not have been possible. Tell your people that. The GDR people in the protests and demonstrations have been sincere, not aggressive. This makes it very impressive. There have been no conflicts, even though in East

---

[3] Checkpoint Charlie was the nickname for the once tightly guarded gate allowing passage between East and West Berlin.
[4] Egon Krenz was the last leader of East Germany.
[5] An avenue in West Berlin.

Berlin, Leipzig and Dresden hundreds of thousands have been in the streets. I hope they will continue to be calm and peaceful. This is my short report.

The President: First, let me say how great is our respect for the way the FRG [West Germany] has handled all of this. Second, my meeting with Gorbachev in early December has become even more important. I want to be sure you and I spend enough time on the telephone so I have the full benefit of your thinking before I meet with him.

Kohl: We should do that. It's important.

The President: I will call Brady[6] today or tomorrow to tell him of your suggestion for a rapid completion of the IMF agreement on Poland. Fourth, I want to see our people continue to avoid especially hot rhetoric that might by mistake cause a problem.

Kohl: That's very good of you.

The President: Fifth, I want to tell the U.S. press of our talk, that you gave me a thorough briefing, that you did publicly acknowledge the role of the U.S., and that you and I agreed to talk later next week.

Kohl: Excellent.

The President: Take care, good luck. I'm proud of the way you're handling an extraordinarily difficult problem. . . .

---

[6] Secretary of the Treasury Nicholas F. Brady.

Appendices

Appendix A:
Thematic Index

Appendix B:
Study Questions

For each of the Documents in this collection, we suggest below in section A questions relevant for that document alone and in Section B questions that require comparison between documents.

1. George Kennan, The Long Telegram, February 22, 1946

A. Why does Kennan believe the Soviet Union poses a threat to the United States? Why is the Soviet Union so suspicious of the outside world and how do these suspicions shape Soviet foreign policy? What actions are the Soviets likely to take and how should the United States respond? Does Kennan believe the United States should go to war against the Soviet Union?

B. How similar are the policies proposed by Kennan to those proposed in Documents 2 and 6? How do Documents 1, 2, and 6 show the "containment" of communism becoming the centerpiece of U.S. foreign policy? In what ways does Lyndon Johnson use containment as a justification for U.S. action in South Vietnam in Documents 29 and 31? How do Documents 12 and 22 criticize containment?

2. President Harry S. Truman, Special Message to the Congress on Greece and Turkey (The Truman Doctrine), March 12, 1947

A. Why are Greece and Turkey important to the United States? What threats do the two nations face? What does Truman believe the United States should do to help Greece and Turkey? What are the two "alternative ways of life" almost all nations must now choose between, according to the president? Why should the United States help nations and people choose one of these alternatives? Why does the president refer to the costs of World War II in his address?

B. How does the policy recommended by Truman resemble the proposals put forward by George Kennan in Document 1? How are they different? Is the Marshall Plan (Document 3) an extension of the Truman Doctrine? Does Truman believe that aid to Greece and Turkey was the correct action to take when he gives his Farewell Address (Document 14)? In what ways does Document 21 resemble the Truman Doctrine?

3. George C. Marshall, "European Initiative Essential to Economic Recovery" (The Marshall Plan), June 5, 1947

A. What problems continue to bother Europe's economy? What are the required solutions? Why does Marshall believe it is "logical" for the United States to help fix these problems? If the United States doesn't help, what might happen in Europe? Why does Marshall believe Europeans should take the initiative while the U.S. assists? What are the hoped-for outcomes?

B. How closely related are the Marshall Plan and the Truman Doctrine (Document 2)? Is the Marshall Plan a fulfillment of George Kennan's recommendations (Document 1)? Is NSC 68 (Document 6) a break with the approach of the Marshall Plan?

4. Dean Acheson, "Crisis in Asia – An Examination of U.S. Policy," January 12, 1950

A. Why does Acheson believe it is impossible to have a single "Asian policy"? What common factors should the United States consider in its policies in the Pacific and Far East? Why do the Chinese nationalists lose the war to the Chinese communists? Why is the Soviet Union (which Acheson also calls Russia) interested in north China? Why is Japan important to the United States? What is the "defensive perimeter" (that is, a line to defend) the United States should have in the Pacific and Far East? What does Acheson say nations on the other side of the perimeter should do if attacked?

B. In this speech, Acheson defends the Truman administration against criticisms that it is "soft" on communism in Asia – how do Senator Joseph McCarthy and General Douglas MacArthur step up these criticisms in Documents 5 and 9? Does Document 8 show Truman following the policies recommended by Acheson in Document 4?

5. Senator Joseph McCarthy, Address to the League of Women Voters, Wheeling, West Virginia, February 9, 1950

A. Why does McCarthy believe the United States is losing the Cold War? According to McCarthy, who within the United States is helping the communists? What kind of list does McCarthy claim to have? Why might his accusation have attracted lots of attention and controversy? What does he think must be done?

B. How does Robert Treuhaft (Document 15) question the fear and alarm raised by speeches like McCarthy's? How is Document 7 a rejection of the approach taken by McCarthy? Does Document 7 agree with McCarthy on any points? How do the Students for a Democratic Society (Document 22) criticize the widespread fear of communism?

6. National Security Council, United States Objectives and Programs for National Security (NSC 68), April 7, 1950

A. What are the basic purposes of the United States? What are the basic purposes of the Soviet Union? What does NSC 68 predict will happen if the United States and its allies fail to act to stop the Soviet Union? What steps should the United States and its allies take? What advantages and strengths does the United States have?

B. How do the view of the Soviet Union and the threat of communism expressed in this document differ from the views expressed in Documents 1 and 2? How might the outbreak of the Korean War (Documents 8–9) have made NSC 68 appear more credible? How is Document 12 similar to NSC 68?

7. Margaret Chase Smith, Declaration of Conscience, June 1, 1950

A. Why does Smith believe she needs to speak out? What are the "basic principles of Americanism"? What criticisms does Chase make of the Truman administration and the Democratic Party? Why is Chase also critical of her own party, the Republicans? What challenges does the Republican Party face? What is the Declaration of Conscience?

B. In what ways does this speech criticize the tone and content of Document 5? How is the definition of Americanism in this document similar to the American Way defined in Document 6? In what ways are this speech and Document 15 similar?

8. Harry S. Truman, Report to the American People on Korea, April 11, 1951

A. Why is the United States fighting in Korea? What have the United States and its allies accomplished so far? Why hasn't the United States directly attacked

China? What are the risks of expanding the war? Why does the president relieve General MacArthur of his duties in Korea?

B. How do Truman's explanations of the purposes of fighting in Korea show the policy of containment (Documents 1–3) being applied? In what ways does this document show the influence of Document 6? Does Truman appear to be responding to critics who accuse the administration of not doing enough to fight communism (Documents 5 and 7)? Does Truman seem to expect General Douglas MacArthur (Document 9) will criticize him too?

9. General Douglas D. MacArthur, Address to Congress, April 19, 1951

A. What is at stake in the Korean War, according to MacArthur? What does he think must be done to win the war? Why is communist China such a great threat to the United States and the rest of the world? In what ways is MacArthur critical of the Truman administration's conduct of the war? Does he praise the administration in any way?

B. In what ways is this speech a criticism of the policies outlined by Secretary of State Dean Acheson in Document 4? Do MacArthur's recommendations provide the "boldness" called for by John Foster Dulles in Document 12? How is MacArthur's view of communism similar to the view expressed in Document 6?

10. Judge Irving Kaufman, Sentencing of Ethel and Julius Rosenberg, April 5, 1951

A. Why does Kaufman believe the Rosenbergs are guilty of a crime worse than murder? What problems have resulted because of the help given to the Soviet Union? Do you think the couple's death sentence is too harsh? Why or why not?

B. How do Documents 5 and 7 make similar statements about the danger of espionage? Do Kaufman, McCarthy, and Smith exaggerate the threat of spies?

11. U.S. State Department, The Negro in American Life (Guidance for the Voice of America), February 5, 1952

A. What themes or topics does the Voice of America (VOA) emphasize in its coverage of African Americans? How does the VOA handle the topic of civil rights? Why do you think the VOA carries lots of statements by African

Americans who are critical of communism? How does the VOA handle news of attacks and violence against African Americans?

B. Does this guidance show an early effort to present the United States as a nation committed to protecting human rights in the ways described by Jimmy Carter in Document 40? How might VOA features on African Americans have advanced the purposes of containment as expressed in Documents 1, 2, 3, and 6?

12. John Foster Dulles, "A Policy of Boldness," May 19, 1952

A. Why is Dulles so critical of containment? What does he propose as an alternative? What does he believe are the advantages of "boldness"? How can allies help the United States? Why does Dulles believe threatening to use nuclear weapons is a good policy? Does he admit any risks of such a policy?

B. How does the stalemate in the Korean War (Documents 8–9) influence this article? Is the 1956 uprising in Hungary (Document 17) an example of the liberation of people living under communist rule that the United States should attempt? Does Document 11 show the Voice of America being used in the ways Dulles wants? Is Document 43 also a call for liberation? If so, how?

13. Federal Civil Defense Administration, Organized Evacuation of Civilian Populations in Civil Defense, June 12, 1952

A. What kind of evacuation does the policy propose? Who is responsible for carrying out the evacuation? Who do you think the "priority groups" for evacuation might be? Why doesn't the policy provide details about how to evacuate?

B. Would this policy help make the "policy of boldness" in Document 12 more acceptable to Americans? Why or why not? How does Document 22 show fears about nuclear war?

14. Harry S. Truman, Farewell Address, January 15, 1953

A. What does Truman say about the Cold War? Which policies carried out during his presidency does he mention? Why do you think he chooses to bring them up? Why he is optimistic that the United States will triumph over communism? What is communism's basic failing? What possible ways could the Cold War end?

B. How does this speech compare to President Eisenhower's Farewell Address (Document 19)? What are the major similarities and differences? How do other presidents emphasize the cause of worldwide freedom in their speeches (Documents 20, 27, 31, 40, and 43)?

15. Robert E. Treuhaft, Testimony before the House Committee on Un-American Activities, December 3, 1953

A. Why does Treuhaft believe he has been called before the committee? Why is he having so much trouble finding an attorney to represent him? Why does he believe the committee's actions are damaging to the Constitution and to the country? Is Treuhaft ignoring the threat communism poses to the nation?

B. Are Senator Joseph McCarthy's speech (Document 5) and Judge Irving Kaufman's sentencing statement (Document 10) examples of the "hysteria" Treuhaft believes is spreading across the country? Are committee hearings an effective way to uncover illegal communist activity? What are the similarities between Treuhaft's testimony and Document 7?

16. National Security Council Directive, NSC 5412/2, Covert Operations, December 28, 1955

A. Why does the National Security Council believe the United States should undertake covert (that is, secret) operations? What are such operations supposed to accomplish? What types of operations are planned? Why does the National Security Council believe the United States should hide or deny its sponsorship of these operations?

B. Are the plans and operations described in Documents 24, 35, 38, and 39 examples of the covert operations called for by the National Security Council? What are the potential positive and negative results of covert operations? In Document 40, why does President Carter criticize the use of covert operations?

17. Dwight D. Eisenhower, Radio and Television Report to the American People on the Developments in Eastern Europe and the Middle East, October 31, 1956

A. What happens in Eastern Europe after World War II? Why hasn't the United States used force to liberate Eastern Europe? How is the United States now responding to the Hungarian uprising? What does the United States hope will happen?

B. Is the uprising in Hungary an example of how people could be freed from communism as called for by John Foster Dulles in Document 12? If so, why do you think the United States doesn't directly help the uprising?

18. Richard Nixon and Nikita Khrushchev, The Kitchen Debate, July 25, 1959

A. How does Khrushchev hope the exhibit might improve relations between the United States and the Soviet Union? How does Nixon think Soviet visitors will respond to the exhibit? Why does Nixon believe communication, especially through television, is necessary for both nations? How is Khrushchev's claim that American homes only last 20 years a criticism of capitalism? How does Nixon respond?

B. In Document 1, George Kennan says that the Russian people are eager to know more about the United States: how does the exhibit give them information about Americans? How might exhibits such as this one have supported other international outreach efforts by the United States (Document 11)?

19. Dwight D. Eisenhower, Farewell Address, January 17, 1961

A. What is the basic purpose of the United States, according to Eisenhower? Why must the nation be careful to avoid big increases in defense spending? What does he mean by a "military-industrial complex"? Why is it a hazard to the nation? Why is so much federal support for corporate and university research also a danger?

B. In what ways does Document 22 echo Eisenhower's concerns about defense spending? Compare Eisenhower's speech to Document 42: had Eisenhower's advice been followed by the time Ronald Reagan speaks on the topic of national security?

20. John F. Kennedy, Inaugural Address, January 20, 1961

A. What will the United States do to defend liberty? Why must the United States help end poverty around the world? What are the common "enemies of man"? What does President Kennedy ask Americans to do? What is his request of the people of the world? What does he believe global cooperation and friendship can accomplish? Is this speech a major reshaping of American Cold War goals and policies?

B. In what ways is Kennedy's speech similar to Documents 2, 14, and 19? Are there differences – if so, what are they? In what ways does Document 31 also express optimism and confidence?

21. Dean Rusk and Robert McNamara, Report to President Kennedy on South Vietnam, November 11, 1961

A. Why must the United States take action to stop the spread of communism to South Vietnam? How will a failure to stop communism hurt the United States? What is the main U.S. objective in South Vietnam? What must the United States be willing to do to achieve this objective? How can other nations (especially those in SEATO) help?

B. In what ways does this report resemble the recommendations made in Documents 2 and 6? Does Document 29 show President Johnson carrying out this report's recommendations? Compare the report to Document 32: why do these authors have such differing views on what the United States should do in Vietnam?

22. Students for a Democratic Society, the Port Huron Statement, 1962

A. Why are the students uncomfortable with the world as it is? What problems currently exist in the United States? What kind of new social system do they want to create? How are they critical of American Cold War policies and actions? Do the students see communism as a problem?

B. Compare the students' view of the threat of communism with the views expressed in one of the following documents: 1, 2, 6, 12, or 21. How are the views different? Similar? Why might the students later be critical of the war in Vietnam? What might the students say about the way in which the Voice of America covers civil rights (Document 11) – would they approve of this coverage? How are the warnings about militarization similar to the caution offered by President Eisenhower in Document 19?

23. John F. Kennedy, Statement on Cuba, September 4, 1962

A. Why is the United States concerned about Soviet actions in Cuba? Why does Kennedy believe Soviet action must be considered part of a global challenge to the United States? What will the United States do next?

B. Compare this speech to Document 26: how are they similar? How does this speech show the United States fulfilling the policy of containment called for in Documents 1, 2, and 6?

24. Minutes of the Meeting of the Special Group (Augmented) on Operation MONGOOSE, October 4, 1962

A. Who do you think is the "higher authority" that wants more progress on Operation MONGOOSE? Why does the group want to use Cuban exiles to carry out sabotage against the Cuban government? What problems might "massive activity" cause for the United States? What actions does the group recommend?

B. Does this document carry out the goals of NSC 5412/2 (Document 16)? Compare Document 24 to Document 39: how much do U.S. policies toward Cuba change between 1962 and 1976? Why do you think it is so important to the United States to get rid of communism in Cuba? What other documents in this collection might help answer this question?

25. Central Intelligence Agency, Soviet Reactions to Certain U.S. Courses of Action on Cuba, October 19, 1962

A. Why is the Soviet Union putting missiles in Cuba? Why must the United States force the missiles' removal? What are the advantages and disadvantages of the options (warning or blockade) to get the missiles out of Cuba? How might the Soviet Union respond to U.S. actions? How likely is the chance of an all-out war between the Soviet Union and the United States?

B. Document 6 predicts the Soviet Union will try to dominate the world. Does Document 25 show this prediction coming true? Is the placement of missiles a response to the actions taken by the United States in Operation MONGOOSE (Document 24)?

26. John F. Kennedy, Radio and Television Report to the American People on the Soviet Arms Buildup in Cuba, October 22, 1962

A. What is the threat facing the United States, according to President Kennedy? Why can't the United States and the world accept the placement of Soviet missiles in Cuba? What actions does Kennedy order? Does he fully explain the dangers of the situation?

B. Compare Documents 25 and 26. At the time, Document 25 is classified, meaning that it is not made public; Document 26 is a public speech. What are the similarities in how the two documents assess the placement of missiles in Cuba? What are the differences? In his speech, does Kennedy keep the promises he made in Document 23? Does the Soviet Union's placement of missiles in Cuba show the Soviet Union testing the resolve of the United States as George Kennan predicted in Document 1?

27. John F. Kennedy, Remarks in the Rudolph Wilde Platz, Berlin, June 26, 1963

A. Why do you think President Kennedy came to Berlin to speak? What is the "great issue" between the free and communist worlds? How is Berlin part of this struggle? Why is it so important to protect Berlin?

B. Compare this speech to Document 17: how do both Presidents Eisenhower and Kennedy try to boost the spirits of people living under (or close to) communism? Also compare Kennedy's speech to his Inaugural Address (Document 20) and President Reagan's Berlin speech (Document 43). How similar are these three speeches? What are the major differences? What do both presidents say about the cause of freedom?

28. Limited Test Ban Treaty, August 5, 1963

A. What does the treaty ban? How effective is the treaty? Why might other nations sign this agreement? How might a test ban inspire disarmament initiatives?

B. Do you think the Cuban Missile Crisis (Documents 23–26) motivated the United States and the Soviet Union to draft this treaty? Is the treaty ban a fulfillment of the promise of disarmament Kennedy called for in his Inaugural Address (Document 20)?

29. Lyndon Johnson, Special Message to the Congress on U.S. Policy in Southeast Asia, August 5, 1964

A. Why does President Johnson want a Congressional resolution? What obligations does the United States have in Southeast Asia? What are the main features of U.S. policy? What must the United States do to carry out this policy? How can Congress help?

B. Does this speech show the president following the recommendations made in Document 21? Compare Documents 29 and 30: does the Congressional resolution give the president what he asks for? In what ways does President Johnson further develop the rationale for U.S. military action in Vietnam in Document 31?

30. Joint Resolution of Congress, H.J. RES 1145, August 7, 1964

A. What does the resolution give the president the power to do? Why is this authorization necessary? Does the resolution place any checks or limits on presidential action? What might be the advantages and disadvantages to having such limits?

B. Is the resolution similar to the Truman Doctrine (Document 2) and the Marshall Plan (Document 3)? In what ways? Are there differences?

31. Lyndon Johnson, "Peace Without Conquest," April 7, 1965

A. Why is the United States in Vietnam? Why is President Johnson confident the United States will achieve its goals? What are these goals? Why does Johnson believe it would be disastrous for the United States to withdraw? Why does he work so hard to persuade Americans that the war in Southeast Asia must be fought?

B. Compare this speech to Document 29: how consistent are these statements about the importance of Vietnam and Southeast Asia? Does this speech echo the policies and principles President Truman offers in Document 2? Compare this speech with Document 34: under President Nixon, does the United States still have the same goals in Vietnam as stated by President Johnson?

32. George Ball, A Compromise Solution for Vietnam, July 1, 1965

A. Why does Ball doubt that U.S. forces can defeat the communists? What question must the United States answer, and why must a decision be made now? What is the compromise solution?

B. Why do President Johnson and Ball come to such differing conclusions about the situation in Vietnam? Is Ball rejecting the guiding principle of the U.S. Cold War policy, that the United States must stop the spread of communism? Does Ball's advice reflect George Kennan's advice (Document 1) that the United States must choose carefully where and when it seeks to stop the spread of communism? Does Document 33 show that Ball is correct about the problem of using U.S. forces to fight in Vietnam?

33. Student Nonviolent Coordinating Committee, Position Paper on Vietnam, January 6, 1966

A. Why does the Student Nonviolent Coordinating Committee (SNCC) oppose the war in Vietnam? What criticisms does SNCC make about the U.S. government? What does SNCC ask Americans to do?

B. Why might the SNCC paper have angered President Johnson? Are SNCC's criticisms of the war similar to those of George Ball (Document 32)?

34. Richard Nixon, Address to the Nation on the War in Vietnam, November 3, 1969

A. Why does President Nixon not immediately end U.S. involvement in Vietnam's war when he becomes president? According to the president, how and why did the United States become involved in Vietnam? What peace terms does he propose? Who is holding up an agreement? What is the Nixon Doctrine?

B. Compare this speech to Documents 29 and 31: does the United States still have the same goals in Vietnam in 1969 as it did in 1964 – 1965? Does the Nixon Doctrine show a change to the recommendations of Document 6 regarding U.S. support for its allies? If so, how might the war in Vietnam have brought about this change? Compare Nixon's 1973 speech (Document 37) to this speech: does the United States achieve its goals when the war ends?

35. Henry Kissinger and William Rogers, Telephone Conversation about Chile, September 14, 1970

A. Why do you think certain passages are blacked out before this document is made public? Why is the popularity of Salvador Allende so alarming? What is the United States considering doing in Chile?

B. Compare this document to Documents 16, 24, and 39: how similar are the proposed actions? Why do you think covert or secret operations were appealing to U.S. policymakers? Does Document 38 show the United States carrying out Kissinger's and Rogers's recommendations in Chile? How do secret operations against Cuba and Chile fulfill the U.S. commitment to stop the spread of communism? Why is President Carter critical of such operations in Document 40?

36. Joint Statement Following Discussions with Leaders of the People's Republic of China (Shanghai Communiqué), February 27, 1972

A. Why does President Nixon make a trip to China? How do the leaders of both China and the United States find the visit beneficial? What does the United States state as its basic position on the international situation? What does China state as its position? How do these statements differ? What do both nations hope to accomplish by maintaining contact?

B. In what ways does Document 36 repeat basic U.S. Cold War policies as expressed in Documents 1, 2, 3, and 6? Using Document 34, explain how Document 36 shows the influence of the Vietnam War on U.S.-Chinese relations. Using Document 8, explain how Document 36 shows the influence of the Korean War on U.S.-Chinese relations.

37. Address to the Nation Announcing Conclusion of an Agreement on Ending the War and Restoring Peace in Vietnam, January 23, 1973

A. What are the terms of the peace agreement? Why does President Nixon say that the agreement is "only the first step" to peace? What does he promise the United States will continue to do in Vietnam? Why does he address "special words" to the North Vietnamese, South Vietnamese, and the American people? How do these messages differ?

B. Compare Document 37 to Documents 21, 29, and 34: Does the United States achieve its basic goals in Vietnam as stated in these earlier documents? How do you think Americans respond to the end of the war?

38. Richard Nixon and Henry Kissinger, Telephone Conversation about Chile, September 16, 1973

A. Why are Henry Kissinger and President Nixon upset with the media? Why are both men pleased with what is happening in Chile? Why does President Nixon refer to communist Cuba and its leader Fidel Castro?

B. In what ways does Document 35 reveal that the U.S. had been considering a move against Chile's government for several years? Do Documents 35 and 38 carry out the recommendations of NSC 5412/2 (Document 16)? How does the action in Chile compare to efforts to undermine

Cuba's communist government? (Documents 24 and 39.) Why is President Carter critical of covert operations in Document 40?

39. Washington Special Actions Group, Meeting on Cuba, March 24, 1976

A. Why is the United States considering military actions against Cuba? Why are these officials concerned about what is happening in Africa? What do they believe should be done and why?

B. Compare Document 39 to Document 24: In what ways are the proposed actions against Cuba similar? How do they differ? At the end of Document 39, Henry Kissinger expresses a concern that the United States should not appear weak: what other documents that you have read show the same concern?

40. Jimmy Carter, Address at the Commencement Exercises at the University of Notre Dame, May 22, 1977

A. What are the fundamental values of the United States? How does President Carter believe they can guide U.S. foreign relations? Why is he critical of the Vietnam War? Why should the United States not fear a "new world"? What is this new world?

B. How is President Carter critical of previous approaches to stop the spread of communism? Does his criticism of the Soviet Union resemble other presidents' concerns about that country? Why is he critical of the types of covert actions detailed in Documents 16, 24, 35, and 38?

41. Jimmy Carter, Address to the Nation on the Soviet Invasion of Afghanistan, January 4, 1980

A. Why is the Soviet Union's invasion of Afghanistan a threat to the United States and the world? What must be done in response? What is the United States doing to force the Soviets to leave Afghanistan?

B. Using Documents 8 and 41, compare the responses of the United States to the invasions of Korea and Afghanistan: what are the similarities and differences? How does the basic U.S. Cold War policy of containment influence both responses?

42. Ronald Reagan, Address to the Nation on the Defense and National Security, March 23, 1983

A. Why is it necessary for the United States to increase defense spending? Why is it also important to reduce the level of nuclear arms? How does President Reagan explain the Strategic Defense Initiative (SDI)? Why do you think the Soviet Union viewed SDI as a threat?

B. Compare Document 42 to Document 19: is SDI an example of the military-industrial complex and the scientific elite that President Eisenhower raised concerns about in 1961? Using Document 12, explain how Document 42 shows changes in policies regarding nuclear weapons.

43. Ronald Reagan, Remarks on East-West Relations at the Brandenburg Gate in West Berlin, June 12, 1987

A. How does President Reagan explain the cause of freedom and use the Berlin Wall to point out the threat of communism? Why do you think the State Department doesn't want him to call for the wall to be torn down? Why does President Reagan insist on saying this? Why is the statement so dramatic?

B. How is Document 43 similar to Document 27? Why does President Reagan mention the Marshall Plan (Document 3)? How does he use the Marshall Plan to explain the success of democracy and capitalism?

44. National Security Council, National Security Directive 23, "United States Relations with the Soviet Union," September 22, 1989

A. What does the report say about the U.S. commitment to contain the spread of communism over the last 40 years? How is the policy successful? Why must the United States treat Soviet reforms with caution? What must the Soviets do to earn the trust of the United States? What should the United States do? Does the report suggest the end of the Cold War might be close?

B. Compare Document 44 to Documents 1 and 6: how are these analyses of Soviet intentions and actions similar? Different? How much has the U.S. view of the Soviet Union changed since the late 1940s? Are the reforms taking place inside the Soviet Union the type of changes President Truman hoped for in his Farewell Address (Document 14)?

45. George H.W. Bush and Helmut Kohl, Telephone Conversation, November 10, 1989

A. Why do the Poles need U.S. and European help? What is the scene like at the Berlin Wall? What does Helmut Kohl ask the United States to do? Why does he thank President Bush? What does President Bush promise to do? Does Document 45 show the Cold War coming to an end?

B. Compare Document 45 to Document 14: Do the events in Germany show President Truman's predictions about the possible end of the Cold War coming true? If so, how? How does the fall of the Berlin Wall fulfill the goals of Presidents Kennedy and Reagan as expressed in Documents 27 and 43?

Appendix C:
Suggestions For Further Reading

Belmonte, Laura A. *Selling the American Way: U.S. Propaganda and the Cold War*. Philadelphia: University of Pennsylvania Press, 2008.

Dudziak, Mary L. *Cold War Civil Rights: Race and the Image of American Democracy*. Princeton, N.J.: Princeton University Press, 2000.

Engel, Jeffrey A., ed. *The Fall of the Berlin Wall: The Revolutionary Legacy of 1989*. New York: Oxford University Press, 2009.

Fursenko, Aleksandr and Timothy Naftali. *"One hell of a gamble": Khrushchev, Castro, and Kennedy, 1958-1964*. New York: Norton, 1997.

Gaddis, John Lewis. *The Cold War: A New History*. New York: Penguin Books, 2006.

Hajimu, Masuda. *Cold War Crucible: The Korean Conflict and the Postwar World*. Cambridge, Mass.: Harvard University Press, 2015.

Haynes, John Earl, Harvey Klehr, and Alexander Vassiliev. *Spies: The Rise and Fall of the KGB in America*. New Haven, Conn.: Yale University Press, 2009.

Inboden, William. *Religion and American Foreign Policy, 1945-1960: The Soul of Containment*. Cambridge: Cambridge University Press, 2008.

Kaiser, David E. *American Tragedy: Kennedy, Johnson, and the Origins of the Vietnam War*. Cambridge, Mass.: Belknap Press of Harvard University Press, 2000.

Leffler, Melvyn. *For the Soul of Mankind: The United States, the Soviet Union, and the Cold War*. New York: Hill and Wang, 2007.

Leffler, Melvyn and Odd Arne Westad, eds. *The Cambridge History of the Cold War*. 3 vols. Cambridge: Cambridge University Press, 2010.

Mann, James. *The Rebellion of Ronald Reagan: A History of the End of the Cold War.* New York: Viking Press, 2009.

Offner, Arnold A. *Another Such Victory: President Truman and the Cold War, 1945-1953.* Stanford, Calif.: Stanford University Press, 2002.

Suri, Jeremi. *Power and Protest: Global Revolution and the Rise of Détente.* Cambridge, Mass.: Harvard University Press, 2003.

Westad, Odd Arne. *The Global Cold War: Third World Interventions and the Making of Our Times.* Cambridge: Cambridge University Press, 2007.

Whitfield, Stephen J. *The Culture of the Cold War.* Baltimore, Md.: Johns Hopkins University Press, 1991.